*"Bring the power of God's Love
more fully into your daily life."*

PROPHET DEL HALL

Welcome to Book Three of our *Zoom With Prophet* series. It is a transcript of the August 7, 2021 *Zoom With Prophet* meeting titled *"Meditation Versus Contemplation – Advantages and Differences."*

It also includes some comments from YouTube viewers as well as twenty-five additional testimonies from Prophet's disciples. These add clarity to and show practical application of the Zoom meeting topic of this book.

Cover: Contemplation and meditation have a lot of similarities but over time they take you in different directions, thereby accomplishing different personal goals.

MEDITATION

VERSUS

Contemplation

Advantages &
Differences

Editor: Lorraine Fortier

Assistant Editors: Lynne Hall, Del Hall IV,
Cathy Sandman

Cover Image by shutterstock.com/g/pavelk

Cover Design by Del Hall IV

ISBN: 978-1-947255-13-5

MEDITATION

VERSUS

Contemplation

Advantages &
Differences

PROPHET DEL HALL

"The days of any religion or path coming between me and my children are coming to an end" saith the Lord

December 29, 2013

TABLE OF CONTENTS

Appendix

Part One: "Meditation Versus Contemplation" Transcript

Good to see all of you, thank you for joining this *Zoom With Prophet* today. In the next hour or so I hope to share the differences between meditation and my preferred way to contemplate. Both have advantages but there are some major differences. Once you know the advantages and differences, then, depending on what your personal goals are you can choose the one right for you. I think it will be a good review for all of us to go back and really define how I look at contemplation versus meditation.

I know some of you used to meditate, which is fine, both contemplation and meditation have advantages. Often I hear people use the words interchangeably, which is fine, but I have very specific views of meditation and the advantages of and differences of, versus contemplation. So as I prepared this talk I started going back to the fundamentals, the differences, and the basics of contemplation, which I think all of you on Zoom today do using the HU love song to God, versus meditation using mostly the Om, or Aum. I think when we go back and look at the fundamentals that we have not looked at for a long time, maybe we'll see the advantage of contemplation in a new light. So that's what I'm hoping to do today.

Let me start with meditation, and again I sometimes hear people assume meditation and contemplation are interchangeable, but in my *Spiritual Keys For a More Abundant Life* book I define them — they are different and both have advantages — but definitely different advantages. Meditation is usually focusing on a single point of attention, for example, your breath, types of breathing, a word or phrase, or a mantra. And in my view meditation is mostly focused on self and to relax the body, mind, and emotions, and in this world if people can relax and de-stress and calm the mind and their emotions that is actually healthy for the body, that's a very positive thing to do. So let's look at meditation for example … also with meditation you can believe in God or you do not have to believe in God. For example, Hindus that meditate believe in a God from their view and Buddhists generally do not believe in God — yet they still meditate very similarly. So anybody can meditate. I know people in the United States do, and all over the world, it's probably more common than contemplation, and as I prepared for today I realized the more we understand about meditation maybe we'll see more advantages in the way we contemplate, so kind of going back to the basics. Breathing for example, and I do this sometimes before a HU Sing if I think the group is a little bit stressed, if I want to help them relax, I'll have them do some type of breathing exercise. Generally it's through the nose in meditation, you might focus on your breathing to help you relax — maybe even drop your blood pressure. What I have found that works is slowly taking in a deep breath, holding it for a few moments, and then slowly letting it out. Once in a while I'll do that in our HU Sings, contemplations, to help people relax, but that's pretty common in meditation, different types of breath control, and you focus on the breathing, not focusing on the stresses of the day, the job, relationships — you get your mind off worldly matters, which is a positive.

Another aspect of meditation is using a word or a phrase — and a phrase some use, and I like this quote, "I am calm, peaceful, and fulfilled," and in meditation you might repeat that over and over for a while. But eventually most people that meditate get into, after they do the breath control which is beautiful and maybe a word or phrase to help them focus, then they will usually use a mantra. The mantra often used worldwide is mostly related to Hinduism and Buddhism, but people all over the country use it, the world use it, is Om O-M or actually Aum A-U-M, chanting Aum or Om is very common and it can be very beneficial. Doing the breath control, repeating the word or phrase, and doing a mantra like Om can help the body relax and maybe over time get some enlightenment or some insight — but it's mostly focused on self, calming the mind and emotions and the body. And there are some health benefits because if the mind, and there's a connection between the mind and body and I may or may not be able to cover that today, if the mind relaxes often the body will relax, and when you do deep breathing, hold, and then let it out slowly often people will notice their shoulders relax, their hands relax, so there can be a lot of benefits to meditating.

Meditation to me is more passive than contemplation. Once you do all these things and you relax, and maybe form certain body positions or certain hand positions that all have different meanings, sometimes I think people hope something good will come into their consciousness, maybe some spiritual enlightenment, something. You are kind of sitting there waiting for something to "fall in your laps" that will bless you, but even if you do not get an insight you're relaxed, you're not thinking about the stress of the day and that can be a good thing. So anyone can do that type of meditation whether you believe in God or not, and it may relax the muscles, might lower your blood pressure, a lot of good benefits. If somebody who has never meditated starts to meditate often, and they're not interested in contemplating, I think that is a growth opportunity and probably a good thing for them. Anytime we can calm our mind a little bit and our emotions, that's a good thing.

In meditation, some will do this some do not, but some that are serious about their meditations will use yoga positions. They may sit a certain way, for example cross their legs, or have certain body postures, and that's very important to them. They also may hold their hands, and there are many different ways, they'll hold them like this sometimes, you see I'm touching my pointy finger, the index finger, and thumb a certain way, but there are all kinds of ways in meditation to hold one's fingers and hands. And what that does, in theory, it balances out the different energy systems in the body. These are things we do not talk about in contemplation because when we contemplate by singing HU it's all taken care of for us automatically; we do not have to really be concerned about energy systems of the body. But if you meditate and you don't practice the contemplation we do, there are all these different hand positions and postures that will, potentially, will balance out certain energy systems, parts of the body centers, and those are generally called chakras. Again there is a whole lot of stuff going on in meditation that when I get to how we contemplate, it's all done automatically for us, we don't have to do it, and there are other reasons we don't focus on body position which I'll get to. So in meditation there's a whole lot of self-focus, it's not so much focused on God, and it's fairly passive. You have your mind focused on a mantra, your breath control, sitting and holding your hands a certain way. If this kind of meditation helps you to relax and maybe get some insights or some peace I'm all for it — compared to not doing it, any type of meditation I would say is a huge improvement and well worth the time and effort.

Let's get into contemplation, the advantages of contemplation. Contemplation is similar to meditation in that we relax, which benefits the body, mind, and emotions. We start by singing HU, we use the HU love song to God rather than Om, and we can stand or sit or walk, we're not so concerned about body or hand positions but generally sit comfortably in a chair, and we put our hands in our lap. One can also lie down and sing HU when contemplating, however, there is a bit of a challenge not to fall asleep, so if you don't want to fall asleep you might want to sit in a chair. But we do not focus on ourselves — we focus on God — that is one of the fundamental differences of contemplation versus regular meditation. Also, our chakras, our energy systems and centers, and our body positions do not matter to us so much. Sometimes if I feel a group that I am guiding in a contemplation is not relaxed I will have them do a little breathing exercise to relax. I see no problem bringing in some of the meditation techniques of breathing to help people relax for a few moments. I may also suggest the repeating of a saying or phrase that helps bring peace and calm, and then let it go and get into our contemplation by singing the HU love song to God.

Another important part of contemplation in my view, and this is how I define it, contemplation is definitely a form of prayer. Meditation for the Hindus that believe in a God, which I'll explain more later, for them that might be a form of prayer, for a lot of Americans that just want to relax, unwind, stretch, and sing Om, it may or may not be a prayer. But when we contemplate we are definitely in prayer because our focus is not so much on self, our focus is on God, and the physical self is pretty much taken care of when we focus on the Divine. When we contemplate our express goal is to draw close to God, and in the Bible it says draw nigh to God and He will draw nigh to us. So we draw nigh by singing our mantra, we have a mantra just like in meditation, but instead of Om it's specifically HU, a love song to God. When we sing HU we are focusing on sending love and gratitude to the Heavenly Father, but while we're doing that our body generally is relaxed, our emotions generally relax, so we get a lot of the same physical benefits as people doing meditation, but that's not our focus, our focus is in drawing close to the Heavenly Father. By focusing outside of ourselves on God, rather than towards self like in meditation, we benefit from rising above many issues that affect our quality of life.

Sometimes we may go into contemplation wanting to have clarity about a certain topic. For example, we might want better understanding of a dream, or help with a decision we need to make, or perhaps about a relationship or a house you want to buy or a job you want to accept, whatever, but once we go into the contemplation we drop that focus. We might start the contemplation with a desire for information, but once we start the contemplation, which we do by singing our mantra HU, we let it go, we surrender it then we just focus on God, and if we're supposed to get an answer or insight we'll get it during the HU or when we sit quietly after the HU — or maybe in a dream or the next time we take a shower or next time we're relaxed. The answer may come the next day or two or three or maybe a week later, but generally we will receive an insight. So the benefits we receive by contemplating can help with life's questions and become more permanent and have more lasting value than just relaxation in the moment. We're building a relationship with the Heavenly Father, and perhaps His Prophet, and we're receiving spiritual nourishment. I think receiving these benefits is more likely when we contemplate. That spiritual nourishment has lasting consequences, positive ones, as we nourish our eternal self, Soul. Soul makes better decisions in life generally than our physical self. Soul has been around for a very long time while our lower self, physical self, has just been around for however old we are. So as we receive that "daily spiritual bread" it brings more permanent benefits to us than just a relaxed mind and calmed emotions and maybe lower blood pressure. We do not focus on the energy systems and centers in our bodies, chakras, because when we sing HU we trust the Divine will take care of that for us so we put all our focus into the contemplation, the way I define contemplation, into doing a very good HU, "HUUUUUUUUUUU." Each HU we focus on, we try to make it a HU, we try to send love and gratitude, and in a way we are focusing on our breath as we sing HU, but secondarily. When I sing HU I get into a rhythm of breathing, relaxed breathing in and relaxed breathing out, so like during meditation breathing is important but it's not the focus, God is the focus and doing the best HU we can during our contemplations. When we focus on God He will respond — that's the bottom line. So by focusing on God rather than self, God will respond, and He takes care of the things that people practicing meditation are trying to achieve like the peaceful, calm mind and emotions and health benefits. By focusing on God, He responds, and we will generally receive those benefits and more. After a twenty-minute HU I think most people find they are very relaxed, they're mentally and emotionally calm. So we get many of the benefits those that meditate get, but I think we get more permanent benefits, and we get spiritual nourishment and maybe some insights to questions by focusing on God not focusing on self. A fundamental difference between meditation, in my view, and contemplation is meditation is about self and contemplation about God, yet we don't lose out because God will take care of the self. And as we trust God more we care less and less about what we get because we get what we need, He takes care of our needs so we don't have to focus on self so much. We might get suggestions during a HU or afterward in the quiet time or a day later or through a dream, things like health issues, relationships, insights on careers, very useful and more permanent benefits I see than just feeling relaxed and maybe low blood pressure for twenty or thirty minutes. We get benefits and guidance on how to make decisions in life and how to understand things in life that will benefit us more permanently than maybe just twenty minutes of being relaxed. I hope you see that. We might get more dreams after a contemplation; God might respond through a dream. So the bottom line is when we focus on God we get a lot of the same benefits as far as the physical, but we also get insights how to run our life that I think are more precious, more valuable, and more permanent and lasting than the benefits you get just during a meditation, and that's a big plus of contemplation.

So in contemplation, like in meditation around the world, we use a mantra like I said and ours is the HU, it's a love song to God. So let's talk ... just for fun let's go back and review the difference between singing HU, a love song to God, and Om, and I think there are less people that sing HU than Om. The vast majority of people that meditate use Om, Om is very popular worldwide, so let's look at the difference and maybe we'll see an advantage of singing HU by comparing an alternate mantra Om, both are okay but I see a very significant difference. So I think it would be good even for you old-timers, we haven't talked about this in years, to go back and review, "Well why don't we sing Om?" I've had students over the years come up to the retreat center that sang Om, I've had yoga instructors come up that taught Om, and then when they tried HU they noticed a difference, and I'll get to that in a few minutes. I think every single person that used to sing Om in meditations and benefited, there're definitely benefits, who started singing HU noticed a difference, so let's review this.

Om is definitely sung much more than HU. For example it's primarily associated with Buddhism and Hinduism. But it's been adopted by anybody who wants to use it, even those who do not know anything about Buddhism or Hinduism. A person might go to a local gym and get into a certain position, put their hands in a certain position, and they'll sing Om maybe not knowing the history of it, but it's primarily associated with Hinduism and Buddhism. Hindus do believe in a supreme being Brahman — it's trinity Brahma, Vishnu, and Shiva. That is a trinity, like the Christian church has a trinity, only very different. Brahman is considered God and supreme deity by the Hindus, so when they are singing Om it's probably a spiritual exercise for them. Buddhists generally do not believe in God so it's probably more of a self-benefit, maybe hoping to receive some enlightenment but maybe not so much spiritual. So you can sing Om and be spiritually oriented or just want to feel better physically and be more calm during a meditation. When you sing HU I think it would be pretty hard to do it, sing a love song to God, if you do not believe in God, so that would be one primary difference.

When you sing Om, that is actually Aum, it's a vibration that focuses on and may tune you in to the third Heaven, even if that is not known about or your intention, all right. There are twelve Heavens that we know of, and if you don't believe in twelve Heavens there's one Heaven with a whole lot of subdivisions, but there are twelve distinct Heavens, and all my students have been through most of those Heavens. When you sing Om you're singing a sound vibration and it may tune you in to the energy of the third Heaven, so when you sing Om the highest you can go, your target is the third Heaven and you generally don't get past that. Now if you get to the third Heaven that's a huge accomplishment. In the Bible Saint Paul knew a man caught up to the third Heaven, so if you get to the third Heaven versus just staying down in the physical world, that's a beautiful accomplishment and it benefits many people. So there's definitely a plus to singing Om for folks that do not have anything else. The third Heaven is where you find philosophies and the general teachings of conventional concepts of God, which is an advantage versus having no concept of God. But the third Heaven is only the Mental Plane, and most of our time at Guidance for a Better Life retreat center we spend in the Heavens above the third when we contemplate, clear up to the twelfth Heaven. So with practice and over time somebody that is really serious about meditating — the body positions, postures, the mantra, the breath control, all that stuff — over time this is an awesome achievement; they could go from a human consciousness, which I'll explain in a minute, to maybe cosmic consciousness.

Now everybody on the planet has a slightly different consciousness. If there're twenty people in the room there are twenty different states of consciousness, but generally, in my book *Spiritual Keys For a More Abundant Life* I have a section on states of consciousness, there're broad bands of consciousness. If there are twenty people all at the same broad level of cosmic consciousness, they are all at slightly different levels, but still roughly in the cosmic consciousness band. So if somebody uses Om and focuses on the third Heaven they may reach the third Heaven in some state of consciousness, perhaps they end up getting some level of cosmic consciousness. That's a wonderful achievement compared to the human consciousness level.

Now in both meditation and contemplation one of the things we're trying to do over time is to grow our state of consciousness, so I want to compare the two. In the human consciousness, briefly, we find the negative passions of the mind such as fear, worry, anger, guilt, greed, lust, most all these problems down here on Earth come from the human consciousness. The human consciousness has very little true freedom, and the negative power generally controls people through these negative emotions. In the Bible the negative power would be called "the liar" or "the thief that comes in the night" to steal your freedom. So when somebody sings Om, whether they realize it or not, they may be tuning in to the energy of the third Heaven, but that's still better than the human consciousness of the physical world. Now cosmic consciousness is a very early stage of enlightenment, and that is quite a growth from human consciousness, so nice job. Meditation may involve controlling the mind's negative passions so you are more in control, maybe make decisions without too much anger, fear, worry, that's definitely an improvement. Using meditation to help control the mind and the intellectual senses is very beneficial and worth the effort. Sometimes one may receive a little bit of the psychic powers, which is a double-edged sword because they are unstable, that could be fun for a while but the psychic is very unstable and it is generally more aligned with the negative power. It's not real spiritual illumination, but it feels like it for somebody that does not have experience with spiritual illumination. So what I'm saying is that through meditation one can get up to the cosmic consciousness and that's a wonderful achievement. If you do not reach cosmic consciousness but stay more in human consciousness yet you relax and make better decisions, you become a little more in balance, you feel a little bit of spiritual enlightenment, and maybe for those that believe in God achieve a little more connection with God and Spirit, that's a wonderful thing, but it's all relative. In meditation if you end up with a deeper awareness of yourself, again that's a wonderful thing. So, so far I'm promoting meditation as a good thing, and compared to nothing it is wonderful, I highly recommend it if you do not have any other practice, I think it will benefit you, and meditation has a lot of health benefits. When you have cortisol and adrenaline running through your body from constant stress, and you can do a meditation chanting Om, or whatever you want, and do breath control and relax, that is definitely good for your body. Maybe you will even live a little longer, age a little slower, and reduce your blood pressure; it's an excellent way to go unless you have a better option.

Those in Buddhism also use Om, unlike Hindus they generally do not believe in God. They do worship Buddha out of respect and as a way to suppress greed, hate, and ignorance, but Buddha is not God, but it is a way to give praise to somebody outside themselves, and that in and of itself is a benefit — when you look outside yourself, so not a bad thing. Buddhists focus mostly on eight steps to reaching the Mental Plane, that's the third Heaven. Mental, mind stuff, that's all Om can get you to whether you're a Buddhist, Hindu, or an American sitting in the gym or in your bedroom meditating, the best you do is get to the third Heaven, and again that's better than no growth. Buddhism believes in suffering, meditation, and spiritual and physical labor. Good behavior is a way to achieve enlightenment and avoid self-indulgence. Well if you get a little enlightenment, which would be cosmic consciousness, and if you're not so self-indulgent like a lot of people are nowadays, can you see that's a thumbs-up, that is a good thing. Soon we're going to get to contemplation, I think you'll see that may be an even better option for some, but it depends what your personal goals are.

Rather than using Om as a mantra, we use HU, an ancient love song and prayer to God when we contemplate. HU like Om is also a sound vibration. Om focuses like I said on the third Heaven. It's like you're aiming for the third Heaven and that is likely the best you're going to do; you may not get there, but over time and if you're serious about meditating you might get to that level of consciousness with a calm mind and intellect. One generally hits what I call a "glass ceiling" at the third Heaven by singing Om. In contemplation that is not our goal, I generally like to get my students above the Mental Plane early on. I like to get them to the fourth Heaven, the Etheric Plane using the mantra HU. Here they begin to trust their intuition. Many of my students have spiritually grown in former lifetimes and are ready for fourth Heaven experiences, so singing Om for them would not be productive and it might take them backward. Also we do not want to focus on the third Heaven when we would rather praise the Heavenly Father and worship the Heavenly Father on the twelfth Heaven, and the HU vibration originates on the tenth and continues to be the sound on the eleventh and the twelfth Heavens. It actually starts on the tenth Heaven, continuing through the eleventh and twelfth Heavens, which we poetically call the Ocean of Love and Mercy. This is the Abode of the Heavenly Father, also called HU, also called Sugmad, also called God, the supreme God. So when we sing HU, this sound vibration, and send love and gratitude we are aiming high, we're aiming for twelfth Heaven experiences. Now we certainly do not always go to the twelfth Heaven, but we aim high and then the Divine, since we focus on the Divine not self, decides where it is best for us to go. Maybe we do not spiritually go anywhere, maybe just receive an insight about our body or health, or an answer to a question, or clarity on a decision we wish to make. Perhaps the Divine takes us to the first Heaven where we get some emotional healing, or the second Heaven to learn something about a past life that would be helpful in this life, or the third Heaven for mental balance. The Divine may choose to take us during contemplation to the fifth Heaven, the Soul Plane, where maybe we'll get an insight about our eternal self, Soul, and sometimes yes we go all the way, with God's Prophet not without, all the way to the Ocean of Love and Mercy and actually have an experience at the Abode of God on the twelfth Heaven. So right there using a different mantra sets us up for a whole different range of spiritual experiences. We might move from human consciousness after singing HU for a while and maybe achieve cosmic consciousness like somebody singing Om and meditating. But if we keep contemplating, like others keep meditating, over the weeks, months, and years we're likely, especially if one has a relationship with Prophet, to go past the third Heaven and experience all the higher worlds potentially achieving much higher states of consciousness. Instead of focusing mostly on our physical body, which will eventually wear out even if it's calmed down a bit, we are focusing more on our eternal self, Soul, and our relationship with God. Okay.

The big difference in the mantra of HU, besides focusing on God, when someone chants Om, I do not believe it helps them tune in to the Holy Spirit. Perhaps people that do it seriously over a period of time, perhaps that is part of their enlightenment, but I absolutely know for certain, and I've been HUing for about forty years, that when we HU it tunes us in to the Light and Sound of God, God's Voice, His Essence, which is also called the Holy Spirit. It makes us more receptive to the Holy Spirit. And how does God give us all His blessings such as insights, guidance, share His peace with us, give us clarity, maybe joy, whatever? He delivers those blessings from the Ocean of Love and Mercy on the twelfth Heaven. How does He get them down to us wherever we are? Through His Voice, through the Holy Spirit, that is the pipeline. So think about it, if we sing HU and we become very receptive to the Holy Spirit, we call it God's Light and Sound, then we are more receptive to His peace, His joy, His clarity, His insights, His healings, whatever He wants to bless us with, those are all gifts of God's Love just manifesting in different ways. If God gives you a wave of peace or a wave of His Love or wave of clarity, those are all waves of Love but in different packages, and with Om you're not as likely going to get it because you're focused on the third Heaven and self, not on God up on the twelfth. It's not to say the Heavenly Father won't reach out to somebody meditating, but our probability by singing HU and focusing on God rather than self or the third Heaven, our probability is very high that He will respond to our HU prayer. And I would say from years of experience every time we contemplate, whether you recognize it or not, if you sing HU from the heart and send love and gratitude and do a reasonably good HU, that sounds like HU not some other sound, God absolutely will respond. We may not recognize it but He will respond, and if we get no recognition we will get the physical and emotional relaxation similar to meditation without focusing on it, our energy will be balanced, and we're also nourishing Soul, which I don't believe Om can do at the same level if at all. And Soul is our eternal self, and if Soul is nourished It "wakes up" and It can benefit and be an active part of our lives, and we've talked about that before in my talk *Your Magnificent Eternal Self* a few months ago, and there are a lot of benefits to that. That's a whole other topic. (*Your Magnificent Eternal Self* is now available in book form)

The Holy Spirit is the spiritual food we need to grow spiritually as Soul, to "wake up" Soul. So if we HU and we become receptive to It we are absorbing the Light and Sound of God, the Holy Spirit, every time we HU, and that's our daily spiritual bread we need to truly grow, and our growth potential is way beyond cosmic consciousness. You may not grow, but your potential is much higher. First we leave human consciousness with all the passions of the mind behind, which we have talked about before. In my video "Blocks to Spiritual Growth Part One" I talk about how with one's heart full of fear or worry or anger or guilt, any of those, you grow past that with the HU and help of Prophet, then eventually pass through cosmic consciousness if you have not already. By the time you find Prophet you've probably already been past that level even if you're not aware of it. So, and again we don't use postures or certain finger positions, it's not necessary because that's taken care of, the Divine takes care of it. When we focus on the Heavenly Father He takes care of whatever we need, and we get the physical benefits of meditation. When you sing HU it's a lot like bathing in or showering in God's Love, which is unmatched with any other mantra. I don't think there is and I'm not aware of, but I don't believe there's another mantra other than HU to where you literally are bathing in God's Love or showering in

God's Love while you sing HU, and I would rather have that than my blood pressure drop. But frankly, when you're singing HU you're bathing in God's Love, His Spirit, His Holy Spirit, so generally your blood pressure and your health benefits, along with a calm mind — you'll receive all those anyway. So I think we get everything one receives from meditation is what I'm saying, plus the spiritual advantages of contemplation. I truly believe we get pretty much everything somebody does when they meditate, but by focusing on God and singing HU for our mantra we have so much more potential, so we're not missing out. Okay. I think that's important, we're not missing out on anything that I'm aware of that people receive when they meditate. So if we get everything they get from meditating, but we open up and we aim spiritually higher to the twelfth Heaven, and we get all this other stuff — we're nourished, we're bathed in God's Love — I would say that's a significant advantage to contemplating.

Let's say you are trying to decide something in your life. It could be about your career, you want to better understand a dream, about a relationship, a health issue, whatever. Years ago my students would start a contemplation with a desire for clarity on a topic of interest. Perhaps they wanted a better understanding of one of God's Spiritual Keys or a Bible verse. Before contemplation one might ask, "Heavenly Father I'd really like to know more about such and such." Or, "Is this the job that's really right for me?" Or, "Is this the right person to be in a serious relationship with?" And we can still do this, there's nothing wrong with having a contemplation seed in our mind and then start HUing. However, we surrender that question completely, God can remember while we are HUing, He can multitask, I don't think we can. It's better if we not focus on our question while singing HU. We "planted the seed," we asked for information or clarity or guidance or peace or whatever, and then we focus totally on singing the best HUs, every single HU, not just the overall twenty minutes or however long you sing, but every single, specific HU. You, with practice, will realize there's a certain breath control like in meditation that goes with singing HU, and you get into a certain rhythm of breathing in and breathing out. During the HU you might get an answer, during the five or ten minutes after singing where you're just listening to whatever God wants to say, remember it's about Him more than us. Just sit quietly, enjoy the enlightened state you're in, you'll be in an elevated consciousness. An answer might come in a dream or it might come a day or two later. Or you may not get an answer, maybe God decides or Prophet decides you don't need the answer right now, give it more time for whatever reason, but we still benefited, we are relaxed, we're calm, we're peaceful, our body benefited, and we bathed in God's Love. So if we do not receive an answer we still benefited, and we'll get the answer when it's time. God and Prophet know when we need the answer, maybe we need to think about it a little bit more or maybe it's not the right question. So if you do not receive an answer to your "seed question" …

and Jorge in our audience today had a question about this, I'd say getting an answer is the least of your concerns, and being bathed in God's Love and drawing close to God is far more important. If you get the answer great, if you don't, don't worry about it. If you really need it God will give you the answer.

Now years ago we would do a contemplation that way, and if you have something in your heart you want to figure out I'd say that's still a good start to a contemplation. My advanced students, disciples, have transitioned in the last few years. They so trust the Heavenly Father and Prophet now that often they do not even try to come up with something they want an answer to because what we've found lately when we do what we call a "Service HU," where it's only to give love and we're not asking for anything, the Heavenly Father knows what's in our hearts and if we need an answer He gives it to us without even asking. So you can still do the earlier type of contemplation, a huge benefit I believe compared to meditation. We're actively reaching out to God, asking for insights or solutions or peace or clarity or whatever, where in meditation you just hope something drops into your mind or heart, you just go really passive, a blank slate, and maybe something will come. We're more proactive in contemplation, we can ask and there's nothing wrong with that, and I suggest you do it whenever you want to do it. But we have found over the last few years, and are still finding, by not expressing a question, God already knows the question, even if you don't ask it. He already reads our hearts so if we're sending love to God and He's looking at our hearts, if we need an insight or clarity or whatever we need, what we've found the last two or three years is we'll get it whether or not we ask, if it's important, which is really cool. So you can ask, if you don't ask He already knows what's in your heart so save time, you don't even need to focus on the question but you can do either, either one. But that's definitely more active than passive meditation where you just hope something kind of falls into your brain. [When we do a "Service HU" we are taken care of, but our primary purpose is to pray for others. We send love to God asking that He use some of our love to bless others, if it is His will to do so. In this way people we know and care about, and even people we will never meet, may be blessed. A "Service HU" is a prayer for others.]

So since all of you on Zoom are familiar with Prophet on some level, in the next *Day of Spiritual Wisdom* I'm going to go back and review. We haven't reviewed this topic for many years, and I think the title for those that signed up will be "The Wayshower to God." Maybe I will cover some things some of you after years still don't know about Prophet whether it's me or the next Prophet. And I think some of you newer folks are going to come up to the school maybe the first or second time; I thought it would be nice to get into this topic again and review some and provide some new insights for everyone attending. (*The Wayshower to God* is now available in book form)

All the benefits of singing HU can be increased by inviting God's Prophet to spiritually join your contemplation. Now when we are all in a group together singing HU then I'm physically with you, but when you're home, and I know most of my students do, they ask me as Prophet to join them on the inner. I'm spiritually right there anyway, yeah I'm just standing there twiddling my thumbs, but I'd like to be next to you and singing HU with you. That's usually a benefit, and you all can share later after I'm done talking, maybe in the second hour today if you want to, it's definitely a benefit, and it does not diminish your HU at all, but it also builds and strengthens our relationship. You might become more aware of Prophet, we might have some dialogue, we might spiritually hold hands, whatever. It definitely can improve your contemplation, not only the mantra HU and your focus on God, but if you bring in Prophet that can add something to it, something to think about.

The other thing is you may get a lot of guidance during the contemplation, after in the quiet time, an hour or two later, next time you shower, or in another dream. You eventually get insights and guidance, and I'd like you to share in our second hour together about this. But can there sometimes be a problem with getting insights and guidance if you do not understand the answer or do not have somebody to explain what it means to you? God has a certain language, the "Language of the Divine," that is the term I've coined, and Prophets, whoever the Prophet is, are pretty good at the "Language of the Divine." So maybe when we break and come back some of you can share, you often get all these insights and guidance or experiences or dreams, but if you do not have Prophet or another disciple of mine to help you understand the guidance, what do you have? You still have the nourishment, you still drew close to God, and your body is still relaxed so you're still okay, but the big plus, the big advantage is the HU makes you more receptive to God's and Prophet's help. I can't help you much if you're not receptive. I won't force myself, I'm a Wayshower, I'm not a way pusher or puller. So if you want help and if you want guidance from the Divine the HU is awesome, but if you want to understand the guidance — and that's why we debrief and share so much, it makes a huge, huge difference. So if you bring Prophet in during the HU and you know I'm right next to you, and then you get some insight and it's really clear, the insight, but you don't know what it means, you're clear what it was as far as the download but you don't know what it's telling you — then turn around and talk to Prophet, I'm right there with you. And now you understand the guidance, but you also have the physical benefits; your mind is calm and your blood pressure probably dropped just like with meditation. You're drawing nigh to God and He will draw nigh to you. You're being spiritually nourished — you're bathed in God's Love, a big advantage. If you bring Prophet in now I can help you more, or during the HU maybe I can deliver what you need through His Light because you're more receptive when HUing where it could not be delivered if you had not done the contemplation. There may be gifts God has for you He wants me to deliver, but if you're not contemplating then you're not as receptive and it would be awkward to deliver it, the answer might not be comfortable for you. Yet when your heart is open after you contemplate these gifts from God go down smooth. There's another advantage of contemplation, a lot of gifts are just sitting there unopened until you contemplate and you're receptive enough and raised up in your consciousness enough to understand and accept the gifts, so a whole lot of advantages. Meditation is great to a point, but if you can transition to contemplation why would you ever go back?

And speaking of, years ago there was a student named Dan, some of you know Dan he was a yoga instructor for years, taught Om. I've had other students that would come up, do the hand things and cross the legs and all that and it's wonderful, but we HU at the retreat center. They might as well not come if they don't at least listen to and try what I'm teaching, and they do try. But when they were going home they would ask me should I HU or Om? I'd say, "You decide, you go home to your own house, you decide what you want to do." And over the years I think every single person that I recall, they have free will, over time they give up the Om and they transition to singing HU, and the basic feedback I get is when they HU they realize that they've been bumping into a "glass ceiling." And the "glass ceiling" is what? The top of the third Heaven. Dan, years ago, who was a yoga instructor felt for years with everything he taught people he kept bumping into something like a "glass ceiling," and as soon as he started HUing and he dropped the Om he went right past the "glass ceiling." That's why understanding when you Om you're at best tuning in to the third Heaven. You may not get there, but that's as high as you probably will get. When we sing HU, we're singing to Heavenly Father on the twelfth Heaven. We may not get there but we might, and over time most do or they get pretty close.

So I see a lot of the advantages of HUing, and I think by explaining the way we contemplate versus meditation I hope it's even more potent, the advantages we have from the way we do it. And I'm not knocking meditation, but when you compare them there's a huge difference, a huge advantage of the way we meditate, or the way we contemplate excuse me. See, it's easy to interchange those words, anybody can do it.

All right, oh the other thing, I left it off my note card here. Going back to meditation, certain ways they hold their hands, the posture is very important, and breathing, and all that, that's not important to us; you can do it but it doesn't matter. Why are we HUing and contemplating and coming up and working with Prophet? It's not just about blessing you and benefiting your life tremendously, it's about training you to be a coworker, a servant of God. How much can you serve others if you're sitting in some contorted position focusing on breathing and you can't uncross your legs to talk to somebody? So one of the reasons ... and I don't think we've ever talked about this, we're not too worried about how we sit or where our hands go. I find my hands sometimes when I'm HUing I like to tend to do this [Del puts the palms of his hands together with fingers pointing upward as in prayer], but they can be wherever. We don't have to do any special posture because when we HU over a period of years and have Prophet's help, over time, we want to raise up to that higher consciousness, that contemplative state, not just sitting in our bedroom or our house or in a group, but while we're at work, driving in the car — be careful there a little bit — walking around talking to people, and if we were tied like a chain tying us down to certain body positions, somebody would have to come talk to us when we're in our crossed legs and our fingers a certain way, not that that's bad, but that is not being trained at being coworkers at any reasonable level. If you're doing the contemplations I share, you have the potential to be a coworker for God, and God at His Abode on the twelfth Heaven just ordained many of you at a very, very high level a week ago at our annual Reunion retreat. Now you have to regularly contemplate singing HU so you can walk around while still maintaining a higher consciousness level — that higher contemplative state — and not be tied down to a sitting position or hand position or any of those things. How many have never really thought about that? Give me a thumbs-up. Any thumbs-up there? Thumbs-up, yeah. That's why those positions in yoga and meditation, which are great for the body, good stretching, I could use some of that, but the spiritual side is good to a point for self, it's all about self, and there're benefits, but we want to be able to walk around, drive a car, ride a motorcycle, sit in the car talking to somebody, eat food, and be at that higher level of consciousness, and singing HU silently with Prophet right next to you, blending my consciousness with you so you can be used to greatly bless somebody, that's why we cannot be limited to body positions. Okay. That's a huge plus, but our goals are higher, we aspire to become coworkers with God through His chosen Prophet. [Coworkers for God through His Prophet allow themselves to be used by the Divine to bless others. These coworkers are taught how to pass on what God knows is best for His other children, rather than what the coworker might think is best. It is perhaps the most satisfying and fulfilling attainment for Soul, to serve God by blessing His other children. One of Prophet's great joys is to raise up and train those who wish to become coworkers, in other words, servants of God at a very high level.]

All right, let's see, real quick, we are short of time. Spiritual strength is necessary to have access to the kingdom of God and His direct Love, and under guidance of Prophet you can build spiritual strength, but I'll speed this up a bit for time's sake. But most every … if you follow my exercises I suggest to you, my spiritual exercises, you eventually, over time, you will build spiritual strength and then you'll be more able to travel the Heavens with me, maybe go to the Abode of God and not be wiped out because it's too much. So you need to have strength, not so much physical but spiritual strength, resilience. Every spiritual exercise and every contemplation I have given you, if you go back and look, has the HU in it; it's always in there somewhere. I may have other things added in like the Three-Part Prayer, other contemplations, but everything I suggest to you the HU is involved in there somewhere. So that when we contemplate — even if we add other stuff, not body positions but other things we're thinking about, singing HU regularly will build spiritual strength for you. And I don't believe you get spiritual strength through a meditation, although you build discipline if you do it regularly, you build discipline and focus by meditating and that can bleed into other areas of your life, which is a plus. Good self-discipline and focus are a blessing in all areas of life, and you can get that in meditation. And if you're consistent in doing the contemplations I suggest, you're also building consistency and self-discipline. So there's layer upon layer upon layer if you love God and you believe in God — if you don't, like the Buddhists, it doesn't matter — to do the contemplation like we do. There are huge advantages.

Now I said with Om you could experience cosmic consciousness, and that's certainly better than human consciousness, but when you sing HU over time you can get to cosmic consciousness, but you can also go to the next broad band, Soul consciousness, and Soul consciousness is also called self-realization, and you get that on the fifth Heaven. So if you're aiming at the third Heaven you're not ever going to reach, you're rarely going to reach, the fifth Heaven. God can do what He wants, but generally you're not going to go to the fifth Heaven. If you're focused on the third Heaven, you're not likely to go up to the fifth Heaven. So self-realization is on the Soul Plane, the fifth Heaven, and that's where you know you're Soul, a ball of light and love, you're so much more than your physical body, you're not male or female, it's a whole other world. In our contemplations sometimes our goal is to get there, and I think we get there pretty quick, in fact, folks I've never met personally, physically, I know you personally actually really well, but those that have not even been to the guidance retreat center physically — I accelerated that through the mirror spiritual exercise thing I did what a couple months ago — I actually showed you what you look like to God as Soul. So Prophet can accelerate this greatly, but I only did that because you've been contemplating. If you had stuck to meditation I couldn't have done that, you wouldn't have been receptive, and it would not have been a positive experience. So that was only because the new folks have picked up contemplation, you've been pretty consistent at it, so it's a huge benefit. So your growth really depends on how much you contemplate, within balance, not all day you'll get out of balance, but if you're pretty consistent, daily, then Prophet can unpack a lot of gifts that are available for you a little quicker. And that's why God's spiritual mirror I showed you on the inner worked because you've been contemplating not meditating. So you go to the Soul Plane, that's a higher state of consciousness, you start identifying with the eternal self.

Briefly, the next level is called spiritual consciousness, that's above the Soul Plane but below the ocean — you have to have a Prophet to take you there, and you also need the HU and contemplation so you can be receptive to being taken there — that's when most of the time you're aware of the presence of the Holy Spirit either directly or in the form of Prophet, you know Prophet is always with you. Early on you know it because I say so, you kind of go, okay, but by the time you get spiritual consciousness past Soul consciousness you're pretty much like my advanced students in Virginia, you pretty much always feel my presence, and you're very aware of guidance coming anytime throughout the day or night from the Holy Spirit, which Prophet is, basically a concentrated aspect of the Holy Spirit when God ordains him, that is the part you're focusing on that's focusing on you. You start recognizing God's Love more fully, not just during contemplation but all the time. You see coincidences that maybe were protection, they weren't coincidences they were actually the Hand of God in your life, protection, daily guidance, it's a good level to be at. At this level I can blend my consciousness with you. If you're coworking and you need to help somebody or you're trying to make a decision I can blend my consciousness and give you greater insights if we are close, if we have a loving relationship, and if you've been taking advantage of contemplation by singing HU on a regular basis, getting your daily spiritual bread. I hope even the old-timers are seeing advantages that you hadn't really thought about before.

Okay we're going to go a few minutes over, hopefully okay. And then God-realization, I would say anybody that comes up to the retreat center on the mountain when I start taking them to the ocean, not the first trip or two, maybe the first trip, you become God-realized. That's not God consciousness, but you know firsthand from your own experience that God is real, He's living, He's not on the third Heaven He's on the twelfth Heaven whether you call Him Sugmad or Heavenly Father or God or Lord — beyond all faith and all earthly teachings you know that. You may not have a consciousness past Soul-realization, or cosmic consciousness, but you can also have God-realization so these aren't quite linear. You might know God is absolutely a reality, maybe He even expresses His Love at the ocean to you, but you're still transitioning from Soul-realization to maybe spiritual-realization, and I can work around whatever you need and not follow any particular script, I have a lot of latitude to help you. But you cannot reach any of these levels of consciousness without contemplation and contemplation using the HU mantra, and then invite Prophet to join you, all this is possible. Now God consciousness is beyond the physical senses, that's what Prophets often have, that's what I can share with you so you don't ever really need it, if you get to the spiritual consciousness level I can share my consciousness with you, actually, I could share it with you if you're in cosmic consciousness. There are really no rules here. There are general guidelines, but if we have a good relationship and there's a need to bless somebody, you may be a new student, but if you've been HUing I can share whatever you need even if you don't understand completely the purpose of what I am sharing with you, to bless somebody else. So different consciousness levels, they're generally achieved kind of in their normal order of growth, but to bless somebody God's Love trumps any type of order or karma, and if you want to bless somebody and you're open and you've been contemplating and you trust me, I can blend my consciousness regardless of the level you are operating at to bless another child of God.

So you take contemplation, add the HU mantra, and bring in a relationship with Prophet, that's a big advantage that I don't think there is any other way to get. I don't think there's anything that's more advantageous, I think nothing, I really don't think so. Oh, God-realization is reached at different levels — one you know there's a God, you see a ball of light like ten thousand suns but you can feel the personality or something, and then it becomes very personal where He will take a form you can recognize, you can relate to. It's not just, you know, God-realized in a generic sense beyond faith, beyond any earthly teachings, but it becomes very, very personalized, and you realize you have a personal relationship with the Heavenly Father, that it is absolutely possible, and that's one of the big parts of my assigned mission so we ought to, we have to prove it really IS possible for a serious seeker of God. All of you that have been up to the Guidance for a Better Life retreat center for a number of years, you have a personal relationship with the Heavenly Father, so that is a higher level and more personal version of God-realization, but not God-consciousness.

I just received a question handed to me from Lorraine, our producer. It is from Moira, Hi Moira. Moira, I know you have a background in meditation, you had a question about breathing when you used to do meditation. I do not see any reason why you should not do a breathing exercise early on during a contemplation as you settle in if it helps you relax, then think of something you're grateful for to open your heart, and then start your HU. Generally when HUing we are breathing in and out and you get into a certain rhythm. I'm very aware of my breaths most of the time — I think during the whole twenty to thirty minutes I'm gently focusing on my breathing as I sing HU, but if you want to use some of the meditation techniques to relax that's certainly fine. So the regular singing of HU, often, you know, hopefully daily we sing HU and maybe throughout the day a short HU under our breath silently, like nibbling on some food if you have low blood sugar, maybe HU silently at work or a little out loud driving the car, kind of nibble, but maybe a twenty-minute contemplation daily, somewhere around there on a fairly consistent basis bringing Prophet in. I hope you now see how blessed we are to have this contemplation and the mantra of the HU. We can do everything the same but not have the HU, there are other terms we could sing, there're all kinds of other sound vibrations for the different Heavens, but I like the idea we're always shooting for the top, the twelfth

Heaven, and then the Divine will take us where best or give us the insight that we need, and we surrender where we go and even if we get anything back.

So. I guess what is the punch line? Meditation is focused on self, and self-improvement is a very good thing, there's nothing wrong with that, but I believe we're being self-improved when we do our contemplation, but we have so many other advantages. "What is the punch line?" I've given you a whole lot of things, growth, healings, and higher consciousness are possible, meeting the Heavenly Father, and still getting all the benefits of meditation as far as good health and relaxing and calm mind and emotions. Actually, you get a calm mind during meditation and it might last for a while, but we may get healings that help to maintain our calm mind for long periods of time if we focus on God. You might have anger, fear, or worry and meditate being okay for a while and those passions calm down, and I think there's some long-term benefit for people that seriously meditate, but with the HU and

Prophet and God we can actually get a healing of those negative passions where even when we're not contemplating we still have less fear, guilt, worry, or whatever, fewer anxieties in general. My son Del IV was wondering during our break what is the punch line of all this? He was excited and Lorraine and Lynne all seemed excited about this talk. They kind of knew this information but hadn't really thought about all the advantages of the way we contemplate, the way we pray. Our contemplation is a prayer, meditation I think could be for some like Hindus not so much for Buddhists. I believe it's a prayer that surpasses, in most cases, rote prayers, memorizing stuff, but Del IV was wondering well what's the punch line, and he gave me a thought and I loved it. The punch line is you're building a personal relationship with — this may be the biggest advantage of contemplation the way we do it with the HU mantra over other forms of meditation or lesser forms of contemplation — you're building a personal, trusting, and loving relationship with the Heavenly Father and His chosen Prophet. It's really about relationship, beyond self, and we know from the Bible and other teachings when we focus on self we kind of lose self, when we focus outside of self we actually gain self, and that's a rule I don't want to get into today, but I think most are pretty familiar with that.

So I like Del IV's punch line — it's building relationships, and I think it's the absolute most effective and efficient way to build a relationship, and maybe the only way, to where you can personally experience God's Love in His Presence, for example at the ocean or maybe other places but at His Ocean of Love, and a personal relationship with His chosen Prophet. A Prophet in a long line of Prophets, like Isaiah, Jesus, all this long line of Prophets; it's the same line of Prophets. So I think it's almost self-evident to build a relationship with His chosen Prophet, one who can explain what you are getting when you get your guidance because Prophets know the "Language of the Divine," and introduce you to the Heavenly Father when you're ready, and condition you to be able to do it without being overwhelmed at the ocean, and show you how to be bathed consistently in God's Love. I just think our form of contemplation wins over any type of meditation, but if somebody is not interested in this, then meditation I'm all for, but once you have this form of contemplation I don't see why you would want to go back.

Prophet Del Hall

Transcript from *Zoom With Prophet*, originally called "Advantages of Contemplating."

August 7, 2021

Part Two: YouTube Audience Comments

This *Zoom With Prophet* talk was published on my YouTube channel for my viewers. The following are selected comments that I thought you, the reader, might find interesting and benefit from. I believe these comments add some additional clarity and provide a personal perspective on the topic "Meditation Versus Contemplation Advantages and Differences."

Thank you for this masterful discourse on the differences between meditation and contemplation. You clearly explained how meditation (which has its physical benefits) focuses more so on self and self-improvement while contemplation focuses on God, and when we focus on our Heavenly Father, He responds. Knowing this, we trust He takes care of our needs. This distinction has made all the difference in my life because as you said, contemplation nourishes Soul, our eternal self, so It becomes an active part of our lives. I love how you explained HU which is another name for God and when sung, becomes a love song to God. HU is our prayer and takes us beyond the mantra used in meditation. Singing our sacred HU with love and appreciation to God helps tune us in to the Holy Spirit and this leads us to becoming receptive, and when we are receptive it is like absorbing the Light and Sound of God! When singing HU we are bathing or showering in God's Love, His Holy Spirit. Wow! I am so grateful you taught me HU and now know its value; it is a way for me to give love first, helps me to be more receptive to the Holy Spirit, the light and sound, and to your help, and by inviting you to sing with me makes our contemplation that much more sacred, offering me God's peace, joy, clarity, healings, insights, and His waves of Love which have indeed manifested in different ways in my life. As you said, meditation only can take Soul just so far, but contemplation has the great potential to bring us to the twelfth Heaven, to the Abode of God because of the loving and trusting relationship built with God's chosen Prophet. This is all true for me. I have personally experienced God's glorious Love in His Presence. It is such a beneficial gift to be able to receive daily spiritual nourishment through singing HU, breathing in and out God's Love (giving and receiving love) while in your inner spiritual presence. Under your spiritual guidance, I am continuing to spiritually grow in consciousness and build a relationship with my Heavenly Father. To me, contemplation, singing HU, and my relationship with you, God's true and chosen Prophet fulfills the ultimate quest for God and true happiness. Thank you for preparing and conditioning me to personally experience God's Love for me and for escorting me to the very Heart of God. Thank you for stretching me beyond the limits of meditation and into the lasting benefits contemplation beautifully offers and satisfies. With all my love and gratitude, Moira.

Moira Crodelle

Thank you Moira for sharing how contemplation has brought you to experience God's Love. Blessings, Del

Guidance for a Better Life

I love how you explain that when we contemplate, we do not focus on ourselves, we focus on God. In my experience with you for over twenty years, in doing that consistently, I find that I have been taken care of well beyond what I would have been if I just focused on myself. And in the process, I have developed a beautiful, loving relationship with the Heavenly Father as well. This so beautifully sums up what you teach — simple yet profound and counter to what I believe most people focus on. Thank you for sharing this with others — for me, it is a huge part of the foundation, built over time, which has changed my life.

Chris Comfort

Yes Chris, by focusing on God we get the physical and mental relaxation benefits of meditation but also build a relationship with the Heavenly Father. Thank you for this reminder. Blessings, Del

Guidance for a Better Life

Thank you, Prophet, for teaching us how it is possible to be in a state of contemplation all day, ready to serve God as a servant of His at any moment, not just during those times when we are sitting still in a state of prayer, contemplation, or meditation. I have found it very helpful to sing HU quietly under my breath while I am at work, something which I learned from you and never would have thought to do back when I thought one had to be sitting still, preferably with eyes closed, in order to focus on the Divine. Today I sang HU quietly while my body was busily pruning plants at my job. I experienced peace and gratitude and appreciation for my job and the gift of being outside in beautiful weather. I was later led to a conversation with a young man who also enjoys outdoor work. I know all of this and more was possible in large part because of making an effort to stay in a state of contemplation, tuned in to the Divine as I went about my day, not just during time in the morning spent in contemplation. Contemplation has truly been an invaluable key to building a relationship with my Heavenly Father and His Prophet. Thank for sharing it with us!

Roland Von der Muhll

Thank you Roland for your comment. You point out one of the advantages of contemplation over meditation in that you were not restricted by body position. Also our focus is outside of us on the Heavenly Father. Generally focus outside of us actually benefits us more than self-focus. Blessings, Del

Guidance for a Better Life

One of the many reasons I love this video is how educational it is. It explains many things that even seasoned meditation practitioners may not be aware of, and when we are more informed, we can make better choices about what is right for us. Although I too once enjoyed certain benefits from meditation, I realize in hindsight it also has its limitations. I like the way you clarify that contemplation puts the focus more on God and our relationship with Him than on ourselves, yet, since God knows us so well, often our needs are taken care of without having to ask. Contemplation has allowed me to build a true relationship with God, which just continues to get better and better. Thank you, Prophet, for bringing us this wonderful discourse!

Laurence Elder

You are welcome Laurence, and thank you for sharing. Blessings, Del

Guidance for a Better Life

This is an amazing discussion on the advantages of contemplation. As you said there are huge advantages in contemplating versus meditating. Thank you for detailing the differences and making it so clear. Singing HU on a regular basis made a substantial difference in my life. I meditated for many years before you taught me about HU. There was no going back to meditation after that. Thank you!

Paul Nelson

Yes Paul, after contemplating by singing HU, a love song to God, going back to meditation would feel uncomfortable and unsatisfying for most people. Blessings, Del

Guidance for a Better Life

As Del noted, I think one of the biggest differences between meditation and contemplation is in meditation I was trying to relax and just de-stress from the ups and downs of the day and in contemplation I am consciously grateful for my many blessings and I am sending love to God as purely and unconditionally as I possibly can and actively inviting God and His Prophet more fully into my life. These daily contemplations help me to grow my relationship with my Heavenly Father and live a more abundant life in love and service with the Divine, according to the ways of God as I am learning and growing to understand them. I appreciate Prophet's loving guidance during these contemplations as I try to walk more gracefully through the challenges of my everyday life. Learning about contemplation has helped me grow spiritually and blessed my life more than I can express.

Jason Levinson

Thank you Jason for sharing your experience with contemplation and meditation. Blessings, Del

Guidance for a Better Life

I love what you said about aiming higher. Singing a mantra to get to the third Heaven sounds like a good deal until you learn that there is more! Achieving a relaxed body, mind, and emotions through meditation is great, but there is much more offered through contemplation, even a personal relationship with our Heavenly Father and His Prophet. Thank you for the HU, teaching me to contemplate, and the opportunity to aim higher!

Jean Enzbrenner

Thank you Jean for reminding us that singing to God on the twelfth Heaven is more satisfying than to the ruler of the third Heaven, while also achieving a relaxed body, mind, and emotions. Blessings, Del

Guidance for a Better Life

Thank you for sharing this video and the punch line, "Building Relationships," Prophet. I have learned from you and your students to ask during contemplation only a couple of things. I ask to be a blessing in someone's life on that day, and I ask Prophet to guide me in what I need to do to draw closer to him and Heavenly Father. When I trust God and His Prophet to guide me, I know I will get exactly what I need. Singing HU is a sacred time to give love and gratitude to God. I am so grateful to have been given the opportunity to know the HU and to have a personal relationship with Prophet. From what I have learned it is an extreme privilege to be able to sing HU and spend time developing a personal relationship with Prophet.

Joey Zabel

Thank you Joey for your comment. Blessings, Del

Guidance for a Better Life

It really touched me how you shared about with contemplation and the mantra HU, how so much is "built in." How the physical benefits are taken care of so to speak without needing to focus on breathing technique, hand position, etc. Thank you for sharing this video.

Kati Miller

Thank you Kati for your comment. Blessings, Del

Guidance for a Better Life

The transition from meditation to contemplation was an important step on my spiritual journey. When I began to sing HU and count my blessings my heart opened with gratitude. I gradually became more aware of and receptive to God's blessings and Love. Furthermore, I eventually began to contemplate in your inner presence. This additional upgrade was huge. I realized that on my own I had only scratched the surface of recognizing and appreciating God's blessings in my life. Contemplation with your inner presence and help allows me to see much more than just the tip of the "blessings iceberg." This has brought me even closer to my Heavenly Father. My loving relationship with Him has strengthened and borne the good fruits of joy, love, deep inner peace, and gratitude in abundance. Thank you Prophet for this powerful gift teaching that has blessed me so greatly.

Irving Kempf

Irv you broke through the spiritual "glass ceiling" by transitioning to contemplation, thank you for sharing your experience. Your experiences broke through the third Heaven, opening the possibility to have experiences with Prophet up to the twelfth Heaven, the Abode of the Heavenly Father. Blessings, Del

Guidance for a Better Life

I really enjoyed Irv's comment about experiencing gratitude during contemplation. I never used to give gratitude any thought — just another word in the English language, and one that I rarely used. Once I began to learn about gratitude and then began to experience it, I've come to realize there is SO MUCH to gratitude. And I believe I'll always be discovering more and deeper layers to gratitude that will allow me to receive ever more blessings and Love from God. If someone is interested in learning more about gratitude they can do so by reading *Spiritual*

Keys For a More Abundant Life. Thank you for sharing this video!

Kati Miller

Yes Kati, experiencing gratitude opens one's heart allowing more love in, both from other people and from the Heavenly Father. It truly is the secret of love as explained in more detail in my Spiritual Keys book. Blessings, Del

Guidance for a Better Life

Those that shared their experiences helped me to remember that I too was a meditator until I attended my first spiritual retreat at Guidance for a Better Life sixteen years ago when you taught me to sing HU and how to contemplate. Meditation did offer relaxation and helped with disciplining my thoughts. When I sang HU though, which is a love song to God, a pure prayer, I felt more active, like my spiritual life was moving forward. I didn't realize it at the time, but I was at the beginning stages of developing a relationship with God and His Prophet, which I didn't know was even possible. Since that time my relationship with God and Prophet continues to grow and has brought more peace, trust, love, and gratitude into my life to such a degree that it's like God breathed new life into me. Thank you Prophet for these blessings!

Sam Spitale

Thank you Sam for sharing some of the difference between meditation and contemplation you personally experienced. Both have benefits, but there is a "glass ceiling" spiritually when using only meditation. Blessings, Del

Guidance for a Better Life

Great video and follow up to Advantages and Differences of Meditation and Contemplation — Part One. I really loved hearing friends share their personal practical applications of the teachings and guidance they have received from you and how that blesses and improves their daily lives. What beautiful examples of the Hand of the Divine in our lives. We are truly blessed and I am personally grateful for the love and abundance you have brought into my life! Spending daily time in contemplation with you, Prophet, has blessed my life by keeping me spiritually nourished and bringing more love and peace into my life. When we have more love and peace in our life it can radiate out to our family, friends, and people we interact with every day. In these challenging times, our small corner of the world can become a little more loving, nicer to one another, happier, and more peaceful. Thank you for these Divine Gifts.

Jason Levinson

Thank you Jason for sharing your insights. Blessings, Del

Guidance for a Better Life

When I used to meditate I would sometimes feel more relaxed and at peace, and this was a precious blessing from God. However, once I started contemplating through singing HU to my Heavenly Father and then listening in silence to His Voice a whole new reality unfolded. I started having experiences with the Light of God and was nourished as Soul by the light. When I later learned the value of including the inner presence of God's Prophet in my contemplations, asking him to sing HU with me and guide me, I experienced more of the Light of God but also now the Sound of God, the Heavenly music. My heart became so much more open to God's Love and I was blessed to travel as Soul with Prophet into the higher Heavens of the Kingdom of God. I now was blessed with direct experiences with my Heavenly Father and knowing how much He loves me and wants to bless all His children. Contemplating with Prophet is a precious, priceless opportunity to draw close to God. Thank you Prophet for sharing with me the incredible benefits and opportunities for an abundant life which come with contemplation.

Roland Von der Muhll

Thank you Roland for sharing how contemplation was different for you from meditation. Both have advantages but there IS a difference. Blessings, Del

Guidance for a Better Life

Thank you for sharing this video, I appreciate the refresher on the importance and benefits of contemplation! Ahna's comment about focusing on God during contemplation time instead of focusing on trying to quiet my mind really resonated with me. Focusing on God naturally calms my mind and heart without extra stress and strain. When I am focusing on God and thoughts do pop into my mind, I can usually trust that they are from God giving me clarity or an insight on something instead of my mind chatter.

Thank you for teaching me this significant difference.

Michelle Reuschling

It seems you were more calm when focusing outside of yourself on God. I believe that holds true for most people that move to contemplation. Thank you for sharing Michelle. Blessings, Del

Guidance for a Better Life

In my own experience that I spoke of on the video, it is definitely our relationship with the Divine that is opened up when we transition to contemplation from meditation. When I meditated, my focus was on me and how relaxed I could get with the different parameters measured: blood pressure, pulse, breathing, etc. Then when you taught me to sing of my love for our Heavenly Father, it was as though a different level and focus kicked in, raising me up in the process. The relaxation was even more profound and enduring than before. When I began looking outside myself, I gradually became a better servant of God too and saw more opportunities to serve Him, each time to my own capacity as I grew. My awareness of His Love in my life expanded, too, which is that spiraling upward you have spoken of so often. How true it is as you say, "There is always more!" Thank you for your patience with me as I grew and continue to grow.

James Kinder

Yes James, contemplation has most of the same benefits as meditation plus more. Thank you for sharing the differences you experience. Blessings, Del

Guidance for a Better Life

I enjoy and appreciate listening to the personal experiences from those who shared about the advantages of contemplation which benefits their lives in such an overwhelmingly positive way. I especially like how a lasting peace of mind and heart is often experienced after contemplation. Thank you for teaching us so much about our sacred prayer, HU, and the benefits to singing HU purely with a grateful heart. It is a blessing to be able to put our focus on God and to sing and contemplate with you and within your inner presence. Also, it rang true for me on how being grateful and choosing to be receptive to you has led to an increased love and appreciation for my sacred relationship with God and His chosen Prophet. Truly, your proper instruction has made all the difference in my life and in the lives of many. Thank you Prophet for all your help and love and for caring so much for God's children.

Moira Crodelle

You are very welcome Moira. Blessings, Del

Guidance for a Better Life

Part Three: Disciple Testimonies

In this section I am including twenty-five testimonies from my disciples on the topic of Meditation and Contemplation. I hope these testimonies provide additional clarity on this important topic and show some of the profound benefits of contemplation when using the HU love song to God. My more than seventeen books provide hundreds of additional testimonies showing the value of transitioning from meditation to contemplation.

Freedom Beyond the Glass Ceiling

Meditation is a blessing for many. It can be physically and emotionally balancing and bring some needed peace into the hectic world we live in. Contemplation does this as well. However, it also can help you experience your true eternal self, Soul, and develop a conscious loving connection with the Holy Spirit. Once you taste the true freedom that contemplation can bring you'll never want to go back.

I had lots of unanswered questions about life and my purpose and place in it from an early age. I didn't really understand who I was and did not accept or really love myself. By the time I was in my late teens I was actively looking for more in life and decided to give meditation a shot. I had heard positive things from a friend about a ten-day silent meditation retreat they had tried and was intrigued. From the little I knew about it, I assumed I would probably be more peaceful and maybe receive some kind of enlightenment or something. Maybe it would help me be happier in my own skin. The first retreat was a little out of my comfort zone. It was foreign to me not to interact with other people as we meditated, ate meals next to each other, or walked the grounds during breaks. But eventually I grew to like the quiet and solace of looking inside even though I was surrounded by people. I realized how unaware I was of the thoughts that were always going on in my mind. This particular meditation technique involved not reacting to thoughts or sensations but essentially keeping your awareness continually moving throughout the body. I attended several more retreats over the course of the next few years, and did feel peaceful once the ten days were over. I committed to continuing my morning meditations and this consistency was helpful because there wasn't much in life I was disciplined in at the time. I still felt peaceful after my session in the morning, but it didn't transfer very much into my day. Emotionally I was still restless and pretty much the same as before.

This left me a little frustrated. I felt like I had hit a "glass ceiling." I had experienced some positive benefits, discipline, and some acceptance of what my body was experiencing as I sat cross-legged on the floor. But I felt alone. Was this all there was? My knees could be feeling an aching sensation of discomfort and I could remain peaceful in my mind, but wasn't there more to life than just my mind and body? The mental peace didn't sink much deeper and was fleeting.

Looking back, I recognize I was left asking where is God in this? I knew there had to be more. Even though we did not attend church, I had prayed since I was a child and knew that God was out there somewhere. I felt stillness in my meditation but didn't know or feel closer to God. Furthermore, I felt alone in trying to control my mind and not react to my body. While there were instructors at the meditation retreats, there wasn't guidance on how to integrate the benefits of these meditations into everyday life. Life on the meditation pillow felt separate from the rest of my life. Shortly after this I was led to Guidance for a Better Life and Prophet Del Hall. Here I found the more I was looking for — a conscious, loving relationship with God. This was built over many years through contemplations and retreats guided by Prophet Del Hall and in my daily contemplations and prayer time at home. Each contemplation time was unique. I spent time in gratitude and appreciation and singing HU the beautiful love song to God. And afterwards, I had sacred time listening for insights, clarity, guidance, and more. Each of these are pillars of contemplation: gratitude, appreciation, singing HU, and listening for God's response. Contemplation has been and continues to be an integral key to nurturing my relationship with God and coming to love and accept myself as a child of God.

Through Prophet Del Hall's guided contemplations I began to experience that I am more than my mind and body. I recall one of the first times he led me in a contemplation. We were seated physically, but I experienced the freedom of truly soaring as Soul through the sky. It wasn't just something I was seeing in my mind's eye; I was actually having the experience of soaring like a bird while my physical body remained on the ground. When it was time to come back into my body, I sensed almost like a thump. I wiggled a finger and it felt so heavy. I had just had a glimpse of the more I knew was out there, and now my body felt like a lead weight compared to the weightlessness of Soul. The freedom of moving as Soul is unlike the limitations of matter we experience when we are solely aware of our physical form. The physical form was all I had known in my meditations, but I had a taste of freedom now, and I wanted to know and experience more of this! This experience of freedom stayed with me. I felt like a child exploring this whole new and exciting realm, it was just so liberating. While I still appreciate the freedom of "moving" as Soul, contemplation has brought me deeper freedoms which I hold more valuable. The freedom to know myself by receiving insights from the Divine in contemplations. The blessing of being guided and led home to the Heavens and meet my Maker has brought me a freedom to love, which I treasure. I now love God more, I love myself more, and I love others more.

This freedom as Soul did not just stay in the "spiritual realms." Through Prophet's inner guidance, I received help in how to integrate the two together. During contemplations, I received guidance in ways to improve my health, my relationships with my children and husband, ways to improve my work, and much more. I received truth about things I was doing that held me back and by understanding and knowing myself, I could see why I reacted certain ways and why I had certain insecurities and challenges in loving myself and accepting love. Witnessing God's Love for me helped me love and accept myself over time. The contemplations also nourished and strengthened me as Soul and this profoundly transformed my life as I began to operate as a divine child of God in my daily life and make better choices that aligned with my priorities in life. I was free to make choices that were right for me.

I finally began feeling comfortable in my own skin. While the physical form was like a net, I saw it as a gift now too. A place to learn and grow. When I was solely aware of my mind and body, I felt heavy with judgments, preconceived notions, unknowns, and limitations, but as Soul I have an innate respect for the Divine and God's Creation, including myself.

Contemplation continues to be an essential foundation of nurturing my relationship with the Divine. It extends to and transforms the time between quiet contemplations in a way that meditation did not for me. My experience of contemplation has been profoundly different than my experience with meditation. In meditation I felt largely alone in my struggle to change and control my mental tendencies, in contemplation I receive Divine help. In meditation I felt peace, but not God's Love or true freedom. In meditation I felt stuck in my body, in contemplation I experienced the freedom of who I truly am.

Prophet's guided contemplations at retreats and on Zoom have given me so much more than I dreamed was possible in life and in my relationship with God. It has been a profound blessing to have been taken on guided contemplations and to truly know by firsthand experience that I am more than my mind or body — I am Soul! This is so liberating! I am so thankful to have also experienced and know I am never alone and truly loved, protected, and guided in these experiences and in life itself. This gives a lasting peace way beyond mental stillness and for this I am so grateful!

Written by Molly Comfort

My Journey From Meditation to Contemplation with Prophet

This is a wonderful testimony on the journey from meditation into contemplation. Both have their benefits, but it is very clear after reading this which has the greatest potential to bless those who practice it. Even more so it paints a beautiful picture of something more important — the sacred relationship with the one who teaches those who are interested how to contemplate — the Prophet.

Several years before I attended my first retreat with Del, I was blessed by God with a martial arts instructor who taught me how to meditate. At the time, it was exactly what I needed. I was a college student who had a very restless mind, one who was looking for some freedom from its constant chatter, its worries about the future, and my own tendency to overanalyze things. Through silent meditation, I was able to find some well-needed moments of peace and could feel my body relax in ways it had not done so before, chronic tension in my neck and shoulders gradually being reduced. I also discovered that if I focused my attention on my inner spiritual eye an interesting spiral pattern would sometimes start to form. One evening, while lying down on the ground in the woods engaged in meditation, the spiral pattern became more vivid. The next thing I knew I was out of my body, my consciousness floating a foot or so above it. It was a wonderful feeling, but the moment I started to think about it, I was right back in my body. I did not have a clue at the time as to what had just happened and, try as I might, I was not able to repeat this experience through my conscious efforts at meditating. I did not, at the time, have a living spiritual teacher who could help me understand what I had experienced. The peace and mental calm I continued to experience with meditation certainly blessed me, but neither one seemed to be lasting in their effects. If I became engaged in a conversation or was busy with work of some sort, I would often quickly lose what inner peace, mental calm, and sharpened focus I had been able to experience through meditation.

When I attended my first retreat with Del, everything began to change for the better. I had found in Del a living spiritual teacher who seemed amazingly familiar with all things spiritual in nature. Del painted a picture for us of what life could be like when we had good focus throughout the day, not only when we were sitting still meditating. Del also shared with us a sacred prayer and ancient name for God, the sound vibration HU. I loved singing HU the very first time Del led us in a short HU Sing. I experienced peace enter my heart on a deeper level than anything I had previously experienced through meditation. I knew I had found something precious I had been searching for, the perfect sound vibration, the perfect love song to sing. As I continued to sing HU in the months following my first retreat I felt more alive — I was actively engaged in doing something that improved my life. There was nothing passive about singing HU, in contrast to sitting in silent meditation while waiting for something to happen. With singing HU, God now became a part of my daily contemplations, as I was sending love to Him by singing HU, an ancient name for God. I was not just focused on myself and my desire to be calm and peaceful as I had been while meditating in years past.

As I continued to sing HU, I was also blessed in ways that I had never experienced through meditation or through praying to God when I had attended church services. I experienced deeper levels of peace and started remembering my dreams more often. I also was blessed sometimes with moments of seeing the Light of God! It often came in the form of a flash of blue light, which I came to know is the calling card of the spiritual presence of God's living Prophet. Through learning and practicing one element of contemplation, singing HU, I was blessed with many precious experiences and gifts of Divine love. I started to feel I was being actively guided through life by the presence of the

Holy Spirit with me. There was so much more, however, for me to learn about this spiritual key to a more abundant life.

A turning point in my spiritual journey occurred when, more than six years after my first retreat with Del, I decided I wanted a real relationship with God's Prophet and to have him guide me through life. I got down on my knees and offered a prayer of surrender to God's Prophet, trusting that following him, not other spiritual paths, would be the right way for me to go. Now I started taking more seriously what Del taught his students about contemplation. Prophet is a concentrated aspect of the Holy Spirit whom I had been receiving guidance from as I started anew my spiritual practice of contemplation. Prophet is also the Master Key who can unlock the deeper meaning to all of the spiritual keys he shares with his students and disciples. There was much more for me to learn about contemplation from Del, a true Prophet of God.

There was more to the Spiritual Key of Contemplation and Meditation Del teaches his followers than simply singing HU. Del taught us to think of something we were grateful for before we started to sing HU. When I focused on something I was grateful for, my focus was outside of myself and all of my perceived problems, and my heart became more open to receiving God's Love. The act of focusing on things I was grateful for prior to singing HU also improved the quality of the HUs I sang, as my heart was more open to giving and receiving love. As it became easier to sing a beautiful HU my heart opened even more. I even heard many people sing HU in a dream! It was a stunningly beautiful experience of a Sound of God, one which brought up to the surface a deep love for singing HU, a love deeper and stronger than I ever knew I had within me. I believe God also wanted me to know through this dream how He loves the sound of HU and how it is a precious gift to be able to sing HU with other Souls who love our Heavenly Father. This dream was a key step towards experiencing the joy of having a loving relationship with God and His Prophet.

Del also taught us how we could invite the inner presence of God's Prophet to sing HU with us. As I started to follow his advice and asked the inner Prophet to sing HU with me, a shift in my experience of contemplation occurred. I could feel how Prophet had real reverence for the Heavenly Father as he sang HU with me. This in turn inspired me to try to make my singing of HU pure and properly focused in nature. I did not want my mind to be focused on something other than sending love and gratitude to God and making each HU the best HU it could be. This did not mean I would reject an insight the Divine gave me while I was singing this beautiful prayer, such as, an insight about an issue in my life, but over time my intent more often was to give to God than to seek to get something in return. The inner Prophet never seemed to want to get anything from singing HU as he sang with me, his focus being solely on giving of himself to God from what I could perceive.

On the outer during retreats, Prophet Del also helped us to focus more on giving to God through singing HU than on getting something in return for our prayers. Del corrected me when I was not singing a proper HU made with the right sound to it. I was limited in my capacity to give to God if the sound I gave Him was not truly that of HU. The correction I received from Del was a huge blessing, as without making a real HU when one sings it, one will not receive as much spiritual nourishment in return, the "daily bread" Jesus speaks of in the Bible. Del also helped me to trust God would respond to our prayers and contemplations in the way we needed and when we needed it, whether it was an experience of deep peace, an insight on something we needed clarity on, traveling in spirit as Soul into the Heavens of God's Creation, or something else God knew we needed.

A huge gift, which God gave me through His Prophet, Del, involved his teaching me about the value of listening in silence to the Divine response after singing HU. As he once said to us at a retreat, "Spirit does some of its best work in silence." During my early years as his student, I would often be too quick to get up and start doing something of a physical nature after singing HU. If I was blessed with a memorable experience, I was too quick to open my eyes so I could record it in my journal. As I learned to sit in silence I was gifted with more clarity and insight about decisions I needed to make along with deeper levels of peace and contentment. It was often during the silent part of contemplation that I realized someone I had gotten to know recently was someone it was in my heart to get to know better. It was during contemplation or shortly after it that I often saw more clearly what my true priorities were in life, and how I wanted to spend my time, energy, and money.

It was while sitting in silence after a long HU Sing led by Del that I experienced a deep peace, which I knew was the Peace of the Lord. I realized I did not want to do anything that would lead to a loss of this precious peace God had gifted me with and that it was essential to be aware of whether the decisions I was making were leading to more peace in my heart or less peace. With more peace in my heart, it was now easier to trust God. I learned to trust if I was gifted by the Divine with an inner spiritual experience, I would remember what God needed me to remember of it when it was time to make notes in my journal or share about it during a retreat led by Del. There was no need to cut short the time listening in silence to the Divine response out of fear of forgetting an experience God had given me.

I also developed more self-discipline and patience through sitting in silence after singing HU. The self-discipline to meditate had been a positive thing in my life for sure, but with contemplation I experienced a higher level of self-control, a more keen awareness of my thoughts and the direction they were taking me, an awareness of how I did not want to feed negative thoughts, and awareness of how I could self-correct, something I had to do fairly often when I would get worked up about something I had seen on the news. Self-discipline and patience helped me to maintain better focus while I was going about my day and to make decisions that would lead to greater abundance and freedom in life, such as resisting the temptation to do something that would later lead to a loss of peace. I had my challenges with spending too much money, but my financial situation would undoubtedly have been much worse if I had not developed a certain degree of self-discipline through consistent daily contemplations.

I also learned from Del I did not need to be alone in listening to the Divine response. I could ask to be directly within the inner presence of Prophet. It was different to ask to be within Prophet's inner presence than how I had initially asked Prophet to sing HU with me. By asking to be directly within Prophet's inner presence I was asking to be in the concentrated beam of God's Light and Sound, the Holy Spirit which his inner presence is. I knew Prophet's presence was always with me, sometimes sitting next to me as I sang HU, but now I could be directly within his inner presence as I contemplated, provided I did my part to stay spiritually nourished and live the ways of God which Del was sharing with us. Now instead of Prophet being somewhere nearby in spirit form as I sang HU, I could be directly within a beam of God's Light and Love. With the inner presence of God's Prophet enveloping me in God's Love, all things were possible. While within Prophet's inner presence it was easier to focus intently on making each HU the best sound vibration I could. I was not so easily distracted by mind chatter as I contemplated and could send love and gratitude to my Heavenly Father in a focused manner and listen intently to His response while I sat in silence. In listening intently, it was not that my physical hearing was necessarily any keener, but rather that, while within Prophet's inner presence, my heart and mind were peaceful. While in this peaceful state, I was more alert to and receptive to the Divine response to my prayers. Through the opportunity to contemplate while within Prophet's inner presence, I was gifted with an unparalleled opportunity to receive true nourishment for Soul, one beyond what I had already been so blessed with after singing HU for many years.

I do not believe I can overstate how much of a positive change it was for my life to contemplate with Prophet's inner presence nearby me and to then, after many years of receiving guidance as one of Del's students, be able to contemplate directly within Prophet's inner presence. Both of these changes in how I went about singing HU and listening to the Divine response were a profound change from my life when I used to meditate. When meditation and rote prayers were my primary spiritual practice, I felt I was doing everything on my own except for those occasional experiences with the Holy Spirit. While contemplating with Prophet and then doing it more fully within his inner presence, I was never alone! Even if I did not perceive a response to my singing HU or from singing "Prophet," the time spent in contemplation was still quality time to just be with the Holy Spirit. It was time to just be with Divine Spirit in its personalized aspect as God's Prophet, a presence whose love for me was constant whether I sang HU for an hour or simply for a few minutes, whether my mind started chattering for a few minutes or whether I was calm and peaceful throughout the contemplation. With God's Prophet involved, I knew I was never alone. Whether it was a "good day" or a "bad day," I was never alone.

Through asking to be in Prophet's inner presence and making an effort to recognize his presence throughout the day, contemplation became more than a twenty-minute experience of singing HU and "Prophet" followed by listening in silence for the Divine response. It was now possible to be in a state of contemplation throughout the day, to receive insights from the Divine while raking leaves or pruning bushes at my job, while driving to work, riding the bus, even when in the midst of a phone conversation. When I was a young man, I often felt nervous during conversations, as my mind would race to come up with a proper response to things said by the person I was talking with. While operating in the contemplative state in daily life it seemed like time slowed down when I spoke with someone. It was easier to really hear what a person was saying, both in terms of words and also through nonverbal communication, and to then hear the Divine presence of the Holy Spirit within me guide me in responding in a way that would best serve that individual.

Prophet's inner presence also helped me to recognize the HU in sounds of nature and machines around me and reminded me of the value of singing HU quietly under my breath while busily engaged in a task, all of this helping me to keep more peace in my heart and maintain more proper focus throughout the day. Where I used to be annoyed by certain mechanical sounds or types of music, I now more often heard the HU sound vibration within them. Some days I was more in tune with the Divine than others, but I began to see it was truly possible to be in this focused, contemplative state all day long, which Del had painted a picture of years ago. It was a goal of mine to be in tune with the Holy Spirit and led by it throughout the whole day. It is hard to achieve a goal in life if one does not believe it is possible to achieve it, and it is thanks to Del's presence on Earth I began to see possibilities for spiritual freedom beyond my wildest imagination. Everything Del taught me about contemplation helped me with achieving this goal of being in a state of contemplation all day long, whether it was to focus on something I was grateful for as I started to sing HU, to ask Prophet to sing HU with me, to listen in silence to the Divine response, and eventually, to ask to be directly within Prophet's inner presence.

Del also taught me to not judge my own thoughts. When I used to meditate, I wanted to be free from all thoughts for a while and from my restless mind. I learned from Del how a thought, which came up while I was singing HU, might actually be a Divine response, as God wants to bless me so much He would sometimes gift me with insight on something even before I had reached the point of sitting in silence. Now I am not trying to escape from my mind, but rather seek to operate as Soul, my true self, which has become more active in my life through contemplation and living what Del has taught us. When my true self, Soul, is nourished and active in my life as the result of consistent daily contemplations, I can work with my mind as a useful, valued part of myself that helps me achieve my goals in life. It is no longer working in opposition to Soul. My mind is no longer the enemy, as I used to think of it during my early days of meditation when I would strive to silence it and be free from it. I look forward to contemplating with Prophet every day and to living each day as best as I can in a state of contemplation. It is my intention to do my best to be aware of Prophet's loving presence with me all the while as he guides me, comforts me, and helps me laugh at and learn from my own mistakes and find spiritual strength within me and within his presence — strength that helps me overcome challenges, detach from things I cannot change, change things I can, and so much more.

Not only has it blessed me to learn how to contemplate in ways I never dreamed were possible when I was into meditation, but I have also been gifted with a wonderful way in which to pray for others. Del taught us we could ask our Heavenly Father, if it was His will, to send the love in our HUs to a troubled area or a person it was in our heart to pray for. We would then surrender the outcome of our prayers, it not being our intention to tell God how to fix the planet, or any one of His children, knowing our prayers would be heard and responded to in God's perfect timing. This opportunity to engage in what we came to know as "Service HUs" added a whole new dimension to contemplation. While I could still ask for guidance on a specific topic I needed help understanding or with a challenge I was facing, it was increasingly in my heart to simply want to serve God and His children through sending Him the best HUs that I could, trusting He would bless other children of His however they needed to be blessed. With "Service HUs" it was easier to be fully present with each HU, as I was not looking to get anything in return for my prayers. Now I look forward to singing HU as a way to serve God and His children, and I find real joy in knowing other Souls will be blessed by the love I send to my Heavenly Father. They may be blessed way beyond what I can imagine; Del painted a picture for his disciples of how if we put in a "penny's worth" of prayer through singing HU, our Heavenly Father would add a "million dollars worth" of blessings and bless countless Souls all over the planet. There is no limit to how much our Heavenly Father can multiply the love we send to Him in prayer through singing HU with a grateful heart.

Back when I would meditate, I might be a little calmer and more pleasant the next time I spoke to someone and in that way be a blessing to the person, but with singing HU it is now possible to serve God in helping Him reach His children all over the planet. Could God bless the planet without our help? He certainly could because He is God and capable of anything, but as I learned from Prophet Del, it pleases our Heavenly Father when we reach out to Him in prayer singing HU with intent that our brothers and sisters in this human family of ours on Earth be blessed in some way. Now I do not feel powerless to do anything about the wars and other painful events of life on Earth. Sometimes while singing HU, I have seen with my inner spiritual vision God's Love being sent to children of His in certain countries where I know there is a crisis taking place and immense suffering amid the people. I now feel I am part of the solution to our planet's sometimes troubled evolution. I can now live the Second Commandment to love thy neighbor in ways I did not know were possible before I learned how to contemplate and when meditation was my primary way of trying to connect with the Divine and find peace of mind and heart.

I now enjoy precious moments with Prophet every day in which we express our love and gratitude to our Heavenly Father. I take comfort in knowing someone somewhere on the planet who is hurting in some way will be blessed by the love in the HUs we sing, whether that blessing comes through inner peace, protection from being hurt physically or spiritually, a healing, strength to overcome a challenge or persevere, a warm meal when food is scarce, or clarity about a decision the person needs to make. It is a precious opportunity following a HU Sing to listen in silence to the Divine response and trust, whether or not I perceive a response to my prayers, they are heard and they do make a difference. It is my sincere hope, dear reader, that this testimony helps you to consider giving contemplation a try and to invite God's Prophet or the Holy Spirit, however you may perceive it, to contemplate with you. You may find the Spiritual Key of Contemplation and Meditation adds a whole new dimension to prayer and leads to drawing closer to God in ways you did not think were possible. Contemplation, following the methods Del shares with his disciples has, in my experience, been a key to a more abundant life. It is a life filled with more love, clarity, peace, recognition of truth, and opportunity to serve than I ever dreamed was possible when Del first introduced me to the beautiful sound of HU.

Written by Roland Vonder Muhll

Meditation to Contemplation in Fifty Years

This is another great testimony on the journey from meditation to contemplation and the multitude of blessings making this transition can bring.

In the spring of 1972, I was a junior in college majoring in biochemistry as a premed student. Competition for grades was intense, and I was feeling the pressure. In February of that year an article came out in *Scientific American* about the benefits of meditation on stress reduction. The study outlined the different parameters that were affected positively by meditation: reduction in blood pressure, pulse, and lactic acid in the blood, which is a measure of increased stress in the body. It also pointed to positive changes in brain wave activity in those who meditated. All of this appealed to my scientific mind at the time, and I decided to search out instruction in Transcendental Meditation, or TM for short, the type of meditation studied in the article. I paid my student fee of thirty-five dollars and went through a thirty-minute session of instruction during which I received a two-syllable mantra with general recommendations on how often and when to meditate and for how long each time. It was up to me then to commit to the discipline every day, twice a day if I could. That discipline appealed to me, and I took to the practice as regularly as I could.

I began to notice what I considered positive effects almost immediately, but would they last? There was no instructor or teacher to turn to if I had any questions. But I stuck with it because it seemed to provide a brief oasis of calm, and I believed in the medical benefits that were backed up by the science. There were even occasional times where I would sense movement while I meditated, or what I thought might be an out-of-body experience, but there was little in the way of direction or explanation available for me. I was meditating regularly with a focus on what it could do for me, but I had been brought up in the Christian faith with an emphasis on helping others and loving my neighbor as myself. There was a disconnect somehow in the back of my mind and heart.

After college I spent two years in the Peace Corps in Korea where I dabbled a bit in Buddhism, visiting various temples and reading about their form of meditation. It was a transformative time for me, and I took up yoga for physical exercise to complement the meditation. In my second year I came to a crossroad. I had an offer to stay in Korea in a beautiful temple and study with the monks and meditate, or return to the states to study medicine to be able to help people with illness. The choice was clear and hinted at an outward focus for me which was to blossom further. I did not hesitate to return and jump into medicine in physician assistant (PA) school.

I kept up with my meditation but had discarded my mantra given to me in TM. In its place I found the Jesus Prayer, repeating silently, "Lord Jesus Christ, Son of God, have mercy on me a sinner." The effects seemed to me to be similar, with waves of purple light on my inner field of vision pulsing toward the center and very calming. That led me to a conversion to Catholicism while in PA school, and I latched onto the liturgy and rituals of the church as though I was thirsty for structure in the midst of my clinical rotations. In particular, I was drawn to the Liturgy of the Hours that Catholic monks do, reciting all one hundred and fifty Psalms over a four week cycle. That discipline stayed with me during a second tour in the Peace Corps in the islands of Micronesia.

So I was accumulating all these extra trappings with my meditation — the yoga, the silent sit, and scripture study. I even had a prayer rug that I thought was essential. I could not see how attached I was to all my own rituals. Then with a marriage that was not going how I thought it should, I was putting up a front which was exhausting physically, mentally, and emotionally. Fortunately for me, somehow all that singing and searching and crying out to the Lord in prayer and meditation was going to bear fruit. He had been listening all the while, and my prayers were indeed heard.

Living in Illinois and involved in Boy Scouts with my two sons and my daughter, I became interested in wilderness survival courses and signed up for one in 1996 that seemed like a good fit, in Virginia at a retreat center now called Guidance for a Better Life. Looking back now I can see that the Divine was leading me, and I was listening. On my first visit there I was immediately struck by the beauty of the place but even more by the warmth and presence of the teacher, Del Hall, and his wife, Lynne. The week was about survival skills, but at every opportunity Del wove in a new way for me of looking at life and living. It seemed like he was speaking directly to my heart at a level I had not experienced before. Even though I was still entrenched in all of my rituals, my heart was opening slowly to hear his words of wisdom. There was so much packed into that week with him that I was hanging on his every word. He spoke with a freedom and authority that conveyed truth at the highest level. Then at the end of the week he shared with us a love song to God, the HU, sung out loud to our Creator! As he explained it, singing HU opens our hearts and may lift us up to the perspective of Soul, and over time I have found that is exactly what happens. HU is unencumbered by words and seems to bypass the mind, which was a blessing in itself for me. It also began to bring me out of myself and into a relationship with the Lord, something I had not dreamed was possible, something not really touched on in the Christian churches I had attended.

That was the tipping point from meditation into contemplation, but I did not realize it at the time, halfway between the fifty years from 1972 and today. It was a slow process at first, but as I accepted singing HU to the Lord, I noticed the physical changes were essentially the same as meditation. But as Del often said, there is always more to learn, and now I had a teacher to ask questions of and not wander so much on my own. As I continued to take classes with Del, I had plenty of rough edges of my own, but I kept recognizing the truth in his words, which were always helpful to my spiritual growth. He was unfailingly encouraging and comforting and approachable all at the same time. One of his great gifts to me was clarity about my own life, which was never forced upon me but offered to me to consider and act upon with my own free will.

Way beyond the physical benefits though, I began to see his new way of living was helping me awaken as Soul through nourishing "Soul food." The old meditation had morphed into contemplation with the Lord by singing HU and sending love to Him in a relationship I did not know was possible. My discipline and personal effort helped, but Del's instruction and teaching was invaluable in my practice and growth. I finally had a teacher I could trust and ask questions. Over the years under his guidance, contemplation has become my bedrock and lifeblood without which I cannot live. It is a healing rhythm in my daily life that I cannot do without. My prayer life has been enriched beyond measure and has become more personal with the Lord, something I found I have longed for my entire life but did not know how to experience.

Over the past fifty years my journey has taken me twice to the other side of the world, but I have found my home here in Virginia with a teacher I love from whom I have learned contemplation as a true communion with the Lord. For this blessing of a lifetime and so many others, I give Him thanks and praise.

Epilogue

After I wrote my testimony on Meditation and Contemplation, it felt incomplete, like I had spent more time with my history of meditation than what a difference contemplation was making in my life now. As it happened, one week after I thought I was finished writing, I had an experience that prompted me to add this Epilogue.

I was in Washington, D.C. for a reunion of Peace Corps/Korea volunteers. It had been many years since I had seen these friends, so my heart was filled with gratitude the whole weekend. Del has always taught us that gratitude is the secret of love, and I was feeling it. The gathering was from Friday through Sunday, and on Sunday I got a nudge to leave early that afternoon. My car was parked at the Metro station in the suburbs, and I had taken the subway into downtown Friday night. So I needed to take the Metro back out to pick up my car but didn't know the subway schedule had changed. I went down underground to wait for the right train to catch and waited over an hour before figuring out an alternate route.

The schedule change and long wait could have put me in a funk, but my gratitude sustained me. Just as Del has taught us, I chose to focus on my gratitude and the blessing of being there that weekend. It was an attitude of gratitude and kept my spirits up. When I finally got on the train, I took a seat in the back and sat down.

My daily bread, my spiritual nourishment, is my lifeblood and foundation for living, and I had taken the time that morning in the hotel to sit with the Lord and sing my love song, HU, sending Him love to distribute where He wills. Before singing, I always declare myself to be a perfect vehicle for Him and the Holy Spirit and His Beloved Prophet, but only if God backs me, leads me and guides me, and then I surrender everything back to Him. "I am yours, Lord, do with me as you will," I had said out loud. This is an opening for our contemplation that Del has taught us, to set the stage for our prayers. It gets us out of ourselves and into relationship with the Lord. When we draw close to Him, He draws close to us (James 4:8). That declaration I make each day is not just momentary but lasts throughout the day. So my heart was primed and filled with gratitude to the point of bursting when I sat down on the train.

The subway car was crowded, with most people masked. When the train started up, the noise level grew deafeningly loud. At that moment I began singing HU out loud, mask on, and eyes open. In retrospect it was totally unlike any "meditation" I had done in years past. This was one example of contemplation as Del taught, to be ready in the moment to serve the Lord as His coworker. I had surrendered to Him in prayer that morning, and here was His gift back to me. As I sang, unbeknownst to those around me, I surveyed the carload of passengers. There was a young couple seated to my left, her head resting on his left shoulder. My seatmate on my right was immersed in his computer , oblivious to my singing in the sound of the train. The car was also full of baseball fans dressed in their team colors, young and old, with families talking and laughing among themselves. I lost track of time, pausing my singing to coincide with train stops as people got on and off. I felt like His instrument, His servant, distributing His Love to all those passengers and beyond. With meditation, all these Souls and the noise might have been distractions, but with contemplation everyone and everything served to take me higher and deepen my love for Him and His children.

In the back of each of Prophet's books is a section titled, "Articles of Faith," written by

Prophet Del Hall III. All twenty-six of the Articles are precious to me, but one in particular, Article 15, has stood out from the very first day I heard it. The last sentence says, "… Becoming a coworker with God is our primary purpose in life and the most rewarding attainment of Soul." That sentence articulates something I had always aspired to but did not know was possible or if I could even experience. And this experience of contemplation in the subway is one I can relive, as fresh and inspiring as the day it happened.

Looking back I can see that the advantages of this form of contemplation over meditation are like day and night. It has been a hard-won journey, requiring personal effort on my part, proper focus, and prolonged determination. And it continues to evolve with the help of my beloved teacher, Prophet Del Hall. It is doable in this lifetime, with God's Prophet, for anyone who desires to serve the Lord and puts forth the effort.

Written by James Kinder

The Role of Contemplation in My Spiritual Growth

One of the many benefits to contemplation over meditation is that it can be practiced anywhere at any time. While it can also be beneficial to have a specific time and place to dedicate to nurturing your spiritual connection, there is real freedom in being able to go about your day and remain connected and tuned in.

At one time meditation was one of the better tools available for me to gain a sense of calm relaxation. I obtained similar results through petting my dogs, exercise, or time spent in nature. The effects were beneficial but both limited and temporary compared to contemplation. Meditation did not lead to lasting changes with issues such as fear, anger, worry, and other negative products of the mind. Meditation was not the sacred prayer that contemplation proved to be. Meditation did not help me draw nigh to my Heavenly Father, which was a wish and prayer that lay dormant deep in my heart until Prophet brought the blessings of contemplation into my life. This prayer to have a loving relationship with God was of my true self, Soul. With Prophet's help my heart's prayer could eventually be recognized and expressed to my Creator. With Prophet's help I could recognize and accept the blessings of my Creator's loving response. Contemplation was a key component of the process of Soul's awakening, the stirring in my heart.

Pivotal and lasting growth and change came when I met Prophet Del Hall. He guided me and many others through the transition from meditation to contemplation. His helping hand remains extended to anyone ready to accept his help and guidance to the profound blessings available through contemplation. Prophet taught me to sing HU and practice gratitude by counting my blessings, and to see many blessings from God I had previously missed. The practice of gratitude became the experience of gratitude, which is a direct experience of God's Love. My heart opened more and more to God's Love over time as the process unfolded. Prophet's guidance was a vital component of each step along the way. My love for God grew, and more of His Love flowed into my life, not because I loved Him more but because I had become more receptive to Him. I now know His Love for me was ALWAYS there. I found that I also had more love to pass on to others. By reaching out to my Heavenly Father to know Him better, I expressed the prayer that had long lain unrecognized and unspoken in my heart. Over time as my love for God grew I had more love to give Him through singing HU. During contemplation Prophet has taken me to the Abode of God to see for myself that my HU does indeed go to Him. I have further seen that the love in our HU is purified, multiplied, and sent back as personalized blessings from God to His children, perfect for each Soul. The love I have sent to God has also been returned and blessed me many times over, as is His nature. This is part of God's personalized, loving response. This mutual exchange of love is part of the personal relationship I have long sought.

I was taught by Prophet to recognize and appreciate a wide variety of blessings over the years, much of it done in contemplation. My whole perspective on my very existence has changed through contemplation. All was guided by Prophet as he cleared up misconceptions and pointed me in the right direction towards a relationship with God. I benefitted whether in his physical presence or within his inner presence.

I had profound experiences seeing myself as Soul. As a result I know with certainty I am an eternal, individualized piece of the Holy Spirit made up of God's Light and Sound. Prophet has lifted me all the way to the twelfth Heaven, the Abode of God. My physical body was left safely behind as I was lifted as Soul to meet my Heavenly Father. Previous contemplations with Prophet had prepared and conditioned me for these sacred journeys into the Heavens. Only Prophet is capable and ordained to do so. The sacred prayer of my heart to have a loving relationship with my Heavenly Father has been delivered and answered many times over, and in ways I could never have imagined. I have experienced God's Love and Presence firsthand and come away humbled, speechless, and in awe. I know from experience I am loved and cherished by Him, as are all Souls. Words do not do justice to the magnitude of these experiences and how they have changed my life. To know with certainty that God exists because I have been taken by Prophet to meet Him is a blessing and privilege. To know that my Heavenly Father who is omniscient, omnipotent, and omnipresent loves me just the way I am is an incomparable blessing and gift. I am truly grateful to Prophet who prepared, conditioned, and lifted me in consciousness to make this possible.

All contemplation as a prayer with focus on God is a sacred moment. The joy, peace, love, comfort, freedom, and security contemplation can bring are infinitely deeper and more intense than anything I derived from meditation. I find there is great freedom in focusing beyond myself and instead on God. As Soul I unknowingly have sought this freedom for lifetimes. Soul has lived many, many lifetimes with countless ups and downs. Through lifetimes of experience, Soul has accumulated wisdom beyond the grasp of mind. This wisdom can be more available to us through contemplation. I have freedom from everyday concerns when I view life from the higher perspective of Soul. The concerns do not disappear but no longer get the stranglehold on thoughts and emotions that was the previous norm. In addition, contemplation has provided useful information direct from the Divine. In Prophet's presence my thoughts, ideas, opinions, and insights are of a higher order. Contemplation also brings greater clarity into situations. Taken as a whole these advantages have led to better decisions, which over time have greatly improved the quality of my life. This higher viewpoint and greater sense of freedom are available to all Souls because our Heavenly Father wishes it to be so. He ordained and sent His Prophet to guide us to this higher view of both our life and God's ways. We benefit greatly from both. The limited benefits of meditation pale in comparison.

Another benefit of contemplation is its portability. I am not limited to a meditation space or specific time of day. I can live every moment in some level of contemplation, knowingly connected to my Heavenly Father's Love through my connection to Prophet's inner presence. This brings a solid sense of security and inner peace wherever I go. I can live every moment with gratitude for the blessings in my life. I can live every moment secure in God's Love. I can better live God's ways according to His Four Commandments; through contemplation I know to do so is part of my heart's prayer. My time and effort in contemplation have been richly rewarded with Heavenly treasures. They are more precious and lasting than earthly diamonds. Unlike earthly diamonds, spiritual riches can go with me into future lives.

I have experienced firsthand the boundless advantages and blessings of contemplation. Prophet has taught and proven to me that there is always more to

God's Love in every aspect, so there is more for me to learn about the blessing of contemplation. That is part of the nature of God. His blessings are boundless and beyond full comprehension. I am grateful to know there is more to come in my relationships with both Prophet and my Heavenly Father. I am blessed to know this truth and live daily the joy and gratitude it brings.

Written by Irv Kempf

A Change of Perspective

As a child one generally follows the religious path of their family even if it's not a good fit for them. Often though as they grow older they begin to question if they are where they belong. Some do nothing about it while the hungry follow that call and look for the "more" they deep down know they are missing.

While living at home during my youth I was expected to conform to the religious beliefs of my parents. The church sermons I listened to and the rituals I participated in year after year did not offer me a way to have a clear understanding about the true nature of God, nor did the message I received in church have the effect of encouraging me to draw near to God and establish a relationship with Him. I benefited very little from the doctrine priests provided, and instead, found my Catholic upbringing left me with guilt, fear, and feeling unworthy and separated from God. Deep down I sensed the religious story I heard during the course of my life so far was missing something, but I did not know what.

Once I became an adult and left Catholicism I started exploring other religious paths to broaden my perspective and possibly clear up misunderstandings about God I adopted as a consequence of parochial education. The narrow view I had about the nature of Spirit and the afterlife became quite obvious to me when I read books about people who had near-death experiences and claimed they contacted the spirit world. A degree of skepticism surfaced in me while I studied the stories written about the spiritual adventures of others. Some of what I came across at the time seemed too far-fetched for me to accept, but there was plenty enough believable material available to help open my mind to different points of view and support my feeling there had to be more to existence than what was described by the religion of my youth.

Exploring other people's spiritual experiences ignited my interest and prompted me to take stock and separate my authentic beliefs from those I halfheartedly held on to from my religious training. It turned out my beliefs were relatively straightforward and I felt quite free to explore. I tried some of the rituals, techniques, and meditations I came across in books I read. I thought perhaps the methods of meditation aimed at self-examination, self-exploration, and self-awareness were what I needed to release fear and guilt and live a happy, contented life. Many years trying out differing paths toward "self-discovery" came and went. I had hoped to tap into the states of cosmic consciousness and self-realization gurus and holy men I read about purportedly had access to, but I could not. I still had a sense of uneasiness and deficiency somewhere deep within me where I imagined real meaning and purpose were meant to be. Even so, learning to meditate was a valuable step toward learning to still my thoughts and improve my ability to focus, and I appreciate how meditation helped prepare me for the positive changes in my personal and professional life that came several years later.

I am grateful for the benefits I received practicing meditation roughly twenty years until 2006 when the time came for me to learn the advanced spiritual practice of contemplation. Through God's Grace I had the good fortune of being introduced to contemplation by Prophet Del Hall during a retreat at his school. Unlike meditation, which is mostly about trying to get a better understanding of self, during contemplation our primary interest is placing our attention upon expressing love for God, then as a result, self-centeredness naturally fades into the background. Along with other fundamentals of contemplation I learned to sing the sacred sound vibration HU — God's ancient holy name and a pure prayer to our Heavenly Father. We fill our hearts with love and sing HU to express our gratitude to God for all He is and all He provides. Contemplation is purposeful and requires practice in order to have greater degrees of success with it, but even as a beginner, the positive benefits received from just a short time contemplating were greater than anything I ever experienced meditating, so naturally I put meditation aside for good.

My pursuit to find what I was missing turned out to be a tremendous blessing leading me to God's Prophet. My growing inner and outer relationship with Prophet, along with regular study of scripture, prayer, and contemplation, helped me get to know my Heavenly Father and develop a close-knit relationship with Him too. I am often astounded at my good fortune.

Written by Bernadette Spitale

Our Contemplation is a Prayer

You are a spiritual being, not just a physical body, and it is paramount that the real you, Soul, receive It's daily spiritual nourishment. If nourished, Soul is more receptive and can tune in spiritually to the Holy Spirit. This is critical because this connection is the source of all blessings.

I learned about the sacred prayer of HU from Prophet Del Hall after being led through the gates of his retreat center many years ago. For me, these were the beginning steps to when true living began. HU is an ancient name for God, which is a sound vibration and more than a word. When sung from the heart, it becomes the most beautiful love song to God. HU is so profound, it cannot be summed up in one paragraph as I would come to learn throughout these beautiful years with my teacher, Prophet Del Hall.

Prior to learning HU, I had my favorite prayers which were Psalm 23 and Psalm 139, along with certain songs which spoke to me, but it is HU which helps me purely express my love for God.

With HU, my Heavenly Father hears my prayers, which are wordless and unspoken. Heavenly Father hears and accepts my prayers and then receives my HUs and blesses others as well. HU is a prayer unlike any other prayer, and I am so grateful to have been led to learn, appreciate, and value its gift.

Before being led to and introduced to HU, I had attended Buddhist silent meditations held at a villa run by nuns, which overlooked the Hudson River in New York. I appreciated this early time of learning meditation, which not only helped slow my breathing but helped me to be more aware of my thoughts, aiding to understanding myself a little bit better. I enjoyed this mindful meditation during meals as I ate in silence because it allowed me to be more aware of the tastes and textures of food, and cognizant to what I was feeding my body. Around this time I also started attending classes at Guidance for a Better Life and there Del introduced me to HU and contemplation. So during the next Buddhist meditation retreat, I also sang HU silently, but at the time I did not truly grasp singing HU was feeding Soul and nourishing the true and eternal me.

With HU, I experienced with my spiritual senses seeing light and hearing sounds, which are the twin aspects of the Holy Spirit manifesting. There was a big difference between singing HU and the spiritual experiences I had versus just focusing on my thoughts and their moving in and out of my mind as I would do in meditation. Although meditation helped me to be aware of fleeting thoughts and identify worries and helped me put attention on my breathing to recognize whether it was shallow or otherwise, it was HU that took me past these bodily experiences and the thinking of myself to experiencing true insight, clarity, and understanding.

At the last silent meditation retreat I attended and having already experienced a handful of Del Hall's retreats held in the Blue Ridge Mountains, I knew it was at Guidance For a Better Life retreat center where my spiritual growth had the greatest potential to accelerate. With HU and contemplation, I could go past the thoughts in my head and thinking only of myself and the physical conditions of my body, and focus more on God. With Prophet Del Hall, singing HU and contemplating, which is active rather than passive, takes me past the mental thoughts and the third Heaven to the Soul Plane, the pure spiritual planes or Heavens where I experience myself as Soul, and God's Voice through His Light and

Sound. For me, this was amazing and an answer to my unspoken prayers.

During the last silent meditation retreat, the class gathered in one room and sat on pillows on the floor. The Buddhist monk asked us to chant Aum at the end when our time of silence had ended. As others chanted Aum, a sound associated with the Mental Plane of the lower worlds, I sang HU. I sang HU with love and appreciation for God, knowing it was because of Him I could even breathe. It was God who had given me life and I was grateful for this. I knew there was more than focusing on my breath with meditation, although it was calming to the mind and helpful to my body. With HU, I knew I could be escorted to the higher spiritual Heavens way above the Mental and Physical Planes. When the monk invited us to speak and to share if we chose since we could now talk, I shared how I sang HU during the time of their chanting Aum. I explained HU is a prayer and when sung, it becomes a love song and helps transcend our physical bodies, and as Soul, travel beyond the Physical Plane and into the higher spiritual planes. I expressed how grateful I am to God for the gift of life and His Love. As I spoke, I noticed everyone listened, and there was a stillness in the room. I ended with thanking the kind monk for the quiet and enjoyable weekend and expressed gratitude for their listening. As I was walking to the car, a woman approached me and thanked me for reintroducing her to HU. She said she had heard about HU, the beautiful prayer, at one point in her life and was inspired to start to sing it again. We were both grateful Divine Spirit allowed the opportunity for HU to be heard and shared.

At the time, I knew not what I know now about HU. Many blessings have been given and experienced from singing HU and listening to God during contemplation, which has changed the trajectory of my life. How grateful I am Prophet Del Hall introduced me to HU, taught me the benefits of contemplating, and continues to guide and help me on my spiritual journey home to God. I am also grateful for following my own heart and allowing myself to be receptive to these beautiful spiritual teachings, which offer peace, love, and joy beyond what I could ever conceive was possible. As Prophet promises, receiving daily spiritual nourishment via singing HU and contemplating leads to being more open, sensitive to, and receptive to the Holy Spirit, and with this we become more alert to and aware of Divine guidance.

If it is in your heart, sing HU with an open heart, spiritually look for the Light of God, listen for the Sound of God, and sincerely seek to develop a two-way communication with the Divine. If you desire a loving, trusting, and personal relationship with your Heavenly Father and long to experience your true eternal self, Soul, then yearn no more, for the *Spiritual Keys For a More Abundant Life* shared by Prophet Del Hall teaches truth in which your heart will innately respond and rejoice.

Written by Moira C. Cervone

God's Love Produces Real Results

You are not alone and if you make the effort to draw close to God and Prophet through singing HU daily, God will respond. You will also become more receptive to truth, guidance, and a loving relationship with the Divine, which is the ultimate source of a happy life.

I was anxious and worried as I fretted over my situation. Worry had been my near-constant companion so this was not new to me. But on this particular morning I was aware now that I could ask for help to lessen my anxiety and worry — I could do this by choosing to contemplate and sing HU, a love song to God. I was experiencing a lot of change in my life and with that I found myself even more anxious than usual.

A friend had recently shared a book with me written by Prophet Del Hall that shared the benefits of drawing close to God through contemplation and singing HU. I had read from testimonies written by Del's students how by singing HU they often received guidance and clarity that really made a positive difference in their lives. I was certainly looking for help in my life so for several weeks had been singing HU daily. On this particular morning I chose to sing HU to ask for some help. I had recently quit my job in the veterinary field to start a new career but had just discovered the new career was not what I was looking for and decided to stop pursuing it. Now I found myself needing to return to the veterinary hospital where I had worked to have surgery performed on my cat, and this was causing me a lot of stress. I was not stressed about my cat's surgery, I trusted that would be fine, but what stressed me was the idea of telling my coworkers that I had just quit my new job and had no options for a new job.

At this time I very much valued the opinion of other people. I was having a hard time understanding the changes in my life, and the idea of having to explain my choices to others really frightened me. I knew that rather than trying to "suck it up," to face this fearful situation alone, I could ask for help through contemplation and singing HU. I sat down on my couch, closed my eyes and prayed for help. I didn't know what to ask for specifically, but thankfully we don't need to. God knows us better than we know ourselves and knows what is best for us. I began to sing HU and after ten or fifteen minutes stopped and continued to sit with eyes closed. In my inner vision, for a brief moment, I experienced God's Light. It was a beautiful flowing pink and golden light that brought with it an overwhelming sense of love which brought me to tears. Within this love came healing gifts of clarity and strength. I felt fortified and strengthened, and the idea of facing my former coworkers didn't seem so scary anymore. I didn't necessarily have an answer for any questions I may be asked about my choices in life, but I was free from the burden I felt of needing to do so. I left my house with my cat experiencing more freedom and with more love in my heart.

Arriving at the veterinary hospital everyone was happy to see me and any of the questions I feared may be asked, never were. As I walked out of the building, reflecting on what I had just experienced, tears of gratitude came and also further clarity. While the gift of being able to see and visit with my old coworkers while free from anxiety and worry was a blessing, a greater blessing was revealed to me. This was one of the first times in this life where I was able to experience that making the effort to draw close to God produces real benefits in our lives. We are never alone, and by making the effort to draw close to God and His Prophet by singing HU each day, I become more receptive to this truth and can accept more of the love and guidance that is always available to me. This time together in contemplation and prayer and singing HU, over time, has helped me to build a trusting, loving, and PERSONAL relationship with my Heavenly Father and His Prophet. I can't think of anything more advantageous than that!

Written by Kati Miller

Contemplation Changed My Life

This world is like a prison, a prison of consciousness. Without an experienced guide to show Soul the way Home It is trapped. As Soul gains strength through building a loving relationship with Prophet, and by learning and following the ways of God, the mind will come into alignment with Soul. This allows the two to work together, with Soul free and calling the shots.

When I was growing up my dad meditated and practiced yoga. He followed an East meets West religion, which was a blend between the teachings of Krishna and of Jesus. In the evening he often did yoga, sang devotional songs, and meditated. Over the years I would join him too. He also cooked a lot of vegetarian whole foods. My understanding was the foods and yoga had many health benefits, but they ultimately were to help condition one's body and mind to be calm and able to sit for the long periods necessary in meditation.

At age nineteen my parents gave me a gift to attend yoga teacher training at an ashram in the Catskill Mountains of New York. For a month I practiced yoga for four hours a day and ate a vegan diet consisting mostly of raw foods. I held the vague belief if I could just find the right formula for physical health, this would lead to happiness. There was deep unrest, or really despair, inside of me. This seemed to form around middle-school age and get worse as I got older. My mind mostly worked against me. I was prone to anxiety, worry, and anger. I knew there was a better way to live, but I did not know how. I was searching for something that would provide lasting change and assumed a month of total immersion in yoga would help cease the painful gnawing within me.

In the last few days on the ashram, I had become so limber I was able to do a scorpion pose. I never thought my body could be in such a position. Physically I never felt better, but it did not matter. Each night there was a meditation with devotional singing and silent time. I would attempt to meditate. I would attempt to empty my mind of all thought. I was able to comfortably sit very still. My physical body was not an obstacle, but my experience of meditation was emptier than it had ever been. I thought the yoga and diet would change something about meditating, but for me, it did not.

I went home knowing ashram life and yoga was not my answer. One night sometime after, I had a very vivid dream in what seemed like another world. Everything was blue as if I was seeing through glasses with blue lenses. The landscape was foggy as if I was in the clouds. There was a large castle-like building that had many pointy spires. I worked there, but I did not want to. I seemed to be enslaved by the ruler who was a ruthless being. He was very tall and his head was not shaped like yours and mine. He was having a gathering of powerful people from other faraway places. These people flew in their private jets to where we were. It was my job to gather the keys to their planes and park them like a valet.

This man also had a dog. He kept ordering me to beat the poor creature with a club, which repulsed me, but I did because I was afraid of him. I was very grateful when I woke up from this awful dream.

Four years later I was led by my parents to Guidance for a Better Life retreat center. There I met Prophet Del who extended his hand and his heart to me even though I showed up full of baggage and misconceptions. The spiritual teachings he shared with me seemed to have a similarity to what I knew as a child: reincarnation, spiritual Prophets, but instead of meditation, contemplation. What I knew of these things quickly paled and faded as I experienced unconditional love for the first time through Prophet Del and his wife, Lynne. I did not know at first that my heart's deepest prayer was being answered. It was God's unconditional Love I was craving. I learned through experience, God knew me and loved me all my life. All those years I felt so lost and alone He loved me, but I needed help to learn how to recognize His Love.

Prophet taught me about contemplation which is a way to draw nigh, or close to God. This was completely different than my previous experience with meditation. There were no special poses and no dietary requirements. I learned of the sacred song and ancient name for God, HU, pronounced "hue." This was a loving prayer song to be poured out from a grateful heart to the Lord. Then time was spent in silence, actively listening in case God wanted to share something. Thoughts were not always the enemy but often brought helpful insights. I learned God wanted a relationship with me and this was what I wanted too. He was always communicating and Prophet was teaching me how to understand His Language.

Over the years while attending retreats, Prophet shared God's Light and Sound with his students. He took me and many others to visit the different Heavens spiritually where we were given revelations, healings, truth, and practical help for everyday living. During contemplations, God's Grace, Love, and Mercy literally showered down on me, bathing me in His pure Light and Sound. God's Love became my new foundation, and as I was pruned and purged these spaces were fortified and filled with love.

The truths and insights I received at the retreat center were like seeds. It was up to me to continue to "water the seeds" when I left the retreat center. This was done by spending time in contemplation at home and asking Prophet for help to go deeper with the insights he gave. Answers would often come in the form of dreams, through talking with other Souls, and in countless other ways. Over the years, this active process showed me by experience all life is spiritual. Partitions built in the mind separating and labeling everything began to crumble helping me recognize none of us are ever alone. We are always guided and loved, but we do need help to learn to recognize the guidance. Now, more often than not, I experience the events and interactions of daily life like a continuous stream of giving and receiving love.

Prophet also taught me I am Soul who has a body. When I get into my car, I do not become a car. In the same way, our bodies are a vehicle for Soul to navigate through life on Earth, but we are not the body. When the body dies, Soul continues on Its journey. Prophet's teachings focused on how to nourish and strengthen Soul, the opposite of meditation and yoga, which, in my experience, places more emphasis on mind and body. I learned fear, worry, guilt, greed, and lust are passions housed in the mind. They were negatively impacting my life, but they were not who I was. They are part of the human consciousness, the base state of awareness on Earth, but this state could be transcended with God's Grace, help from Prophet, and personal effort. Instead of focusing on trying to control and clean up my mind, Prophet showed me I could aim much higher, in part by contemplation and singing HU. This was proven to me through experience as Prophet took me, Soul, on journeys into the Heavens.

The sacred sound of HU is also the sound of the twelfth Heaven, the primary Abode of our Heavenly Father. There are many different

Heavens or mansions as Jesus referenced in the Bible. This can be pictured like peeling an onion with each layer representing a different Heaven with distinct characteristics. Each Heaven has a predominant sound and color, and noting this can help one discern where they are in the spiritual Heavens. This information can be helpful to understand one's spiritual experiences with more clarity. The mind is necessary here on Earth to help operate the body, but it is limited in what it is designed to do. Its origin is on the third Heaven and it does not travel beyond to the higher Heavens, but Soul, whose true home is in the Heart of God, is free to travel the higher Heavens if under Prophet's guidance.

Prophet taught me dreams are gifts from God to help us in our daily lives. The startling dream I had years prior started making sense as I began to connect the dots and personal meanings it contained. Blue is the predominant color of the third Heaven which has two parts; the lower governs mental thought and the upper, which is considered the fourth Heaven, governs intuition. The sound for the third Heaven is Aum. The negative power uses the human consciousness as a channel for negativity and the passions of the mind in this world. Dogs had become a personal dream symbol for my mind, which often acted like a stubborn untrained dog. Interestingly the dog belonged to him, but I was ordered to subject it to abuse.

This dream is one example of a multitude of blessings I am appreciative to have received. Many reach the third Heaven through years of meditation and feel it is the final resting place, but they are misled. The negative power is good at its job and provides resistance so we can learn and mature spiritually. What I saw seemed to be truer than what one might typically experience there. It seemed to be beyond the curtain of illusion showing the reality of what was occurring. I do not know how much of what I experienced was metaphorical or literal, but it was enough to give me a reason to not want to align myself with the state of consciousness of that region. I now understand without help, by my own effort of meditating, at best I was paying homage to the negative power, without even realizing this was happening.

Without an experienced guide to show Soul the way Home, this world is like a prison, but as Soul gains strength through building a loving relationship with Prophet and by learning and following the ways of God, the mind will come into alignment with Soul. This allows the two to work together, with Soul in the "captain's chair." With Prophet as my mentor and sacred friend, step by step, like the gradual blooming of a rose, life together has a beauty, clarity, and sense of contentment beyond what I thought could be possible.

Written by Carmen Snodgrass

God's Love Unexpectedly Received

You will never outgive God. Whether it be time, coin, or focus God will not be outgiven. When we dedicate time to draw nigh to Him through contemplation our efforts are more than returned back to us in the form of love, guidance, clarity, comfort, and peace to name a few.

Sleep, that's where I would wind up every time I tried meditation many decades ago when I was in my twenties. I was hoping for some kind of Divine experience from the Creator, as I called my Heavenly Father back then. I tried very hard to empty my mind of thoughts but was not successful. I went to a lecture one time where we were given a three-syllable mantra, not the standard mantra used in yoga. I tried it a few times but would still fall asleep, and the mantra felt creepy. I did not stay with meditation very long and I felt like a failure. Looking back on it now, I do see the sleep as a blessing. I must have really needed some sleep!

In my forties I became a student of Del Hall who began to reveal an ancient, and for most in modern times, "secret" sound, a vibration that when sung was a love song to God, the sacred HU. The focus was not on having an experience but to send love to my Maker, although I often did have experiences. I would start the HU by thinking of something I was grateful for to open my heart. In the early days it was often gratitude for God's chosen Prophet and God's teachings.

The spiritual truths that came through Prophet Del were so nourishing, a depth and understanding of God's ways flowed from him. Over time I became aware that I was receiving spiritual nourishment when singing HU. Though I was not trying to get love, the Heavenly Father was sending love back to me when I sang HU to Him. This gave me more love to send Him! I would feel God's Love as peace or enhanced gratitude, or sometimes as a feeling of love itself. At first I thought I sounded rough when singing HU, I didn't think I had a very good voice. I learned that when I invited God's Prophet to sing with me my HU sounded much smoother. When I sang this love song together with the inner Prophet I did not fall asleep!

I sang HU every day, expecting nothing, I just wanted to sing this love song to God. I knew singing HU was a prayer. After singing HU I would sit quietly with God's inner Prophet and just listen, as Del had taught. Most often I would not get any insights though I didn't feel I had failed. I did, however, receive other gifts such as healings as a result of my contemplations. I also enjoyed the stillness, feelings of peace, and lightness. Being bathed in God's Love was slowly and cumulatively healing me and helping me become more the real me, God's child. I can tell you that if you practice singing HU and invite Prophet to sing with you, well — this could be the start of a beautiful Divine relationship with the Heavenly Father!

Over my life of singing HU I have found there is always more joy, more peace, more awareness of God's personal Love for me, more appreciation for the Heavenly Father, more satisfaction of being able to express myself to Him and for Him, and more awe for this amazing gift of contemplation. I have often received insights later, after my contemplation, as they quietly and freely are given to me as needed. I don't have to strain. I have heard Prophet Del Hall tell students new to singing HU that they may have an experience while singing HU or afterward, but if they do not there is nothing wrong with that. We do not make the experiences we are given them, so there should be no pressure put on ourselves.

One of the differences between meditation and contemplation, with the cornerstone of singing HU, is that HU is a prayer. The Heavenly Father loves to hear our prayers and responds because He loves us. Not only am I blessed from singing HU and contemplating with the Heavenly Father and His Prophet, but my whole family is clearly being showered with blessings. Meditation was me trying too hard to make something happen. The HU and contemplation with

Prophet have helped me build beautiful relationships with Prophet and the Heavenly Father.

Written by Martha Stinson

The Healing Power of HU

HU is an ancient name for God that can be sung quietly or out loud as a love song to God. Singing HU raises you up and opens you up spiritually making you more receptive to receive God's Love and healing. Those that have been singing HU for many years in their daily contemplations know there is always more to experience and learn about HU.

The HU was shared with me about fourteen years ago by my aunt and uncle. The first time I sang it in a group, I wept. It awakened something inside of me. My heart was opening to express pure love to God, and I now know that it was the eternal part of me, Soul, crying tears of joy. I cherish singing HU and have grown to sing it faithfully many times throughout the day. Each time I feel refreshed, more at peace, and more grateful. Sometimes as I sing I am aware of a blessing or an experience and sometimes I am not. Over the years I have received a lot of healing from singing HU.

This summer at a weeklong retreat at Guidance for a Better Life I experienced a profound healing while singing HU. During an opportunity to have alone time at the retreat I hiked to Vision Rock (rock outcropping on retreat center property with a stunning view), sat down, and sang HU. I did not ask for a healing nor did I even know I needed one. I just prayed to give all my love to God and be receptive to whatever and however it came back. I invited Del, the Prophet, whom I trust immensely, to join me spiritually. We met in my inner vision, and to my surprise, we traveled in our Soul bodies above space and time into past and future lives. I had an amazing experience and a healing that penetrated into the past, present, and future all at once. I was shown all the areas of my lives where there had actually been love, but it had not been recognized. I was also shown God's Love flowing into areas that truly were devoid of love. It was both a retroactive and future-reaching healing. To say my past, present, and future received healing during an out-of-body experience might be much for some to accept, but nonetheless, it is true. My spiritual guide, the Prophet, is authorized to do this, and it was the singing of HU that opened me up to receive this blessing.

It is humbling and exciting to know that I cannot grasp the full measure of God's Love, Grace, and Mercy, nor do I need to. This healing showed me that giving my love to God via singing HU came back to me a thousand times over. It is difficult to put words to this healing and what it means to me. It is changing my life for the better and even changing the lives of people around me.

The HU continues to reveal more to me as I grow in my ability to receive God's blessings. I may never comprehend its value completely, but my heart knows that no matter what I go through in life, God's Love can open me to Divine blessings. I know it was the singing of HU that raised me up to a higher level where my spiritual guide could bless me. This blessing would not have been possible without the many years of conditioning my guide spent preparing me for that healing. Without the guide, singing HU alone could not have taken me on the journey of healing I experienced.

I learned from this experience that we all have wounds we may or may not be aware of from this life and even past lives. We all carry a burden equal to our measure. They affect the way we view the world, the choices we make, and our ability to give and receive love. My experience while singing HU gave me more compassion for others and myself. I have always appreciated HU, but now I understand more of its incredible healing power.

Written by Tash Canine

Gift of a New Life

Separation from God and your Divine qualities causes pain of the heart. Many people lead "good" lives but still do not have a "deep peace." It is only when we close the gap and knowingly live a life connected to Spirit that we truly flourish.

Throughout my life I have felt an unfounded doubt and fear that I may not be good enough or able enough to succeed in this life. My life has been blessed by being raised in a loving family that provided me with a good secure home. My parents were supportive of my endeavors and never lost faith in me even during the trying adolescent years when I sometimes did not make the best decisions. I grew into a challenging and satisfying career that provided me with a good income and married a wonderful loving woman who gave me a daughter whom I love dearly. There were many trying times, but things always worked out for the best even when it took time and hindsight for me to realize it.

I had a successful blessed life but still felt fear and doubt and lacked a deep inner peace, until I experienced the healing power of the Love of God. I was introduced to the HU, a love song to God, in 2002 by Del, and throughout the years with his outer and inner guidance, I was being conditioned to be released from the fears I carried for many lives. By singing HU daily and offering my love to God, the Love of God raised my awareness to a level that I was able to accept His healing.

Part of the realization that I was given is that I have not been doing it alone. He has always been with me, guiding me, and providing me with the ability to meet any challenge. I am so loved that I have never been given more than I can handle through His Love and guidance. Each and every life experience is an opportunity to learn, grow, and strengthen my personal relationship with God. Knowing this, my fear and doubt have diminished. A deep peace now fills my being along with the prayer to manifest His Love with every moment of my life. Thank you Lord for the blessings I have been given and continue to receive.

Written by Terry Kisner

I am Soul

You are on a journey of lifetimes to discover the real you, Soul, an eternal spiritual being. One of the best ways to do this is be taken spiritually on journeys as Soul into the Heavenly worlds to experience the real eternal you. As Soul you are loved by your Heavenly Father more than most can understand.

Before coming to Guidance for a Better Life retreat center, I knew I was more than my physical body, but I wasn't sure what that "more" was or exactly what that meant. Prophet Del taught me I am Soul that has a physical body and not I am a physical body that has a Soul. As simple as that statement is, "I am Soul," as words on paper, the profoundness in experiencing and knowing this to be true and truly knowing your real self is amazing. I have been blessed through many years of mentoring by Prophet to experience myself as Soul, to travel the Heavens, visit God's Holy Temples of Learning, and after much conditioning, being taken to the Abode of our Heavenly Father, held in His Hand and experience His Love for me personally. Learning who the real me is has been a journey of discovery and there is still more for me to experience. Your spiritual journey is not a destination or one and done, it is the journey of Soul that takes you through lifetimes in the learning of giving and receiving love and operating as your true self, Soul.

As a spiritual student I was eager to learn the ways of our Heavenly Father and experience the true Love of God, which Prophet was teaching us about and we were experiencing, but it took a while for me to accept and recognize myself as Soul. Prophet not only taught us, but we had the blessing of experiencing for ourselves the principles he was teaching. By experiencing these truths of God they were not just concepts but proven by the reality of the experiences themselves. Before any of our spiritual journey experiences we would be thinking of something we were grateful for which helped open our hearts, and we also sang HU, an ancient name for God. HU is a beautiful prayer that is unencumbered by words and that is simply sending love and appreciation to God our Heavenly Father. We also would give permission for Prophet to take us on these journeys. God gave us free will and Prophet would not go against that so permission was needed if you wanted to participate, and if not, that was fine as well.

Early on in one of my classes at the retreat center I was in a class with several new students I did not know well, and we were blessed by being invited to have a spiritual travel experience. In this inner spiritual travel we were going to experience the freedom of leaving our physical body and flying as Soul. I experienced a freedom that I was not used to, a freedom of boundlessness and lightness. My physical body was safely sitting on a bench in a simple outdoor school room and I, Soul, was flying around with Prophet and experiencing this amazing joy. As Soul I did not have any worries or fears. I just experienced a freedom that I had never had in my physical body. I saw other students flying around and each of them was a ball of beautiful, brilliant, alive light. I had done this exercise before, but this time I noticed something different. Even though the balls of light's outward appearance seemed the same to me, I knew who each one was individually. We had new students and I didn't really know them yet, but as Soul I knew who each one was, recognized them, and I was confident about that. This was a gift from the Divine to give me an experience that my mind could not possibly talk myself out of. Our mind, even though very helpful with the day-to-day running of our life, is not very helpful early on when you are learning who the real you is. To me this was remarkable and started my awareness that we are all unique, individualized Souls.

On another spiritual travel experience, Prophet took the class to visit one of the Heavenly Father's Temples of Learning in one of the spiritual Heavens. God's Temples are places you as Soul can only travel to when you are escorted by Prophet, even if you do not have a conscious relationship with him, know him, or even believe in him — he is still helping you grow under God's direction. In these temples are the pure teachings of our Heavenly Father and are filled with God's Love. In this experience I was invited to explore the temple with Prophet; we entered a room, and in the middle of the room was a beautiful gold-framed, oval floor-stand mirror. I went and stood in front of it, and what I saw was amazingly beautiful. In the mirror I saw myself as this beautiful ball of white sparkling light. It was stunning. There was not a dark spot or ugliness within it. The gold frame that surrounded this mirror and myself was symbolic of God's Love. God's Love was blessing me with the gift of seeing my true beautiful eternal self, Soul. God's Love was surrounding me in the temple and I now know it is always with me.

At this time in my spiritual journey I was having a hard time loving myself. I had a lot of guilt, fear, worry, and pain that I was carrying. These things are not of Soul. They are passions of the mind and the defilements I related to and identified with at that time. In this experience I was being shown in a manner that I could accept; I am not these defilements

I was carrying and holding on to, I am Soul, and I am loved by our Heavenly Father. Prophet patiently mentored me and over time with many God-given healings, experiences of truth, and our Heavenly Father's true Love I started to let go and was healed of these things that limited my freedom and were a wedge between me and the Heavenly Father's personal Love for me.

More recently on a video conference class held over Zoom, Prophet had a special experience for all of us. Again after thinking of things we are grateful for, singing HU, and giving permission we were spiritually handed a special mirror by the inner Prophet and were invited to look into it. When I held up the mirror I experienced the true me — God's Love that I am! I was experiencing myself as God's Love, which Soul is made of. I have been blessed with experiencing God's Love for me many, many wonderful times, but this was so different, this is who I really am! I knew myself and recognized myself not from the perspective of outwardly looking in the mirror but from the inside of being the real me. I also experienced and knew the joy that I am, one of the beautiful qualities of Soul. Our Heavenly Father made Soul out of His Essence of Light and Sound which is His Love, also known as the Holy Spirit or His Voice. Within God's Light and Sound are many Heavenly treasures or qualities: love, peace, joy, clarity, wisdom, truth, freedom, and more.

As I have progressed on this journey I am operating more as my true eternal self and life is abundant in so many ways. Prophet has always told and guaranteed us once we find our true self, we will like what we see. He was right and there is so much more. My hope by sharing this is that you, the reader, might consider starting to explore who you really are, as you are so much more than your physical body. The physical body is necessary here on Earth but it does not have to limit you. The journey with God's Prophet is amazing as you truly discover, experience, and know who you really are. You are a Divine being loved by your Heavenly Father beyond what you can ever comprehend.

Written by Renee Dinwiddie

Skills to Cope With Depression

We all face challenges in life, which are ultimately opportunities for growth. During these times we can actually forge a deeper relationship with and appreciation for God. One key is to not lose sight of the Hand of God that is available. Those that ask God for help and also do their part will ultimately come out stronger, versus just "make it through."

About two years ago my life changed. Everyone goes through changes, but this was one of those major turning points for me. I had recently moved with my husband and two young children to a town where we did not know anyone. The move required that I leave a job I really liked and enjoyed. Then we had our third child. To me this was a whole lot of change in a very short period of time.

I thought I had prepared for these changes. I am not complaining, I have a very good and happy life. I knew all these changes were blessings, but I was struggling. I was experiencing some level of baby blues or postpartum depression, and all the changes added to how I was feeling. This concerned me because I knew depression. I had been depressed at earlier times in my life and did not want to go there again.

Between my personal history and experience from my previous job I had some tools and skills to manage this issue. In the past I did my best to just "make it through" those tough times, but this time was different because I knew the Hand of God was working in my life. I have been blessed to experience God's Love in so many ways. Over the years I have built a loving and trusting relationship with God's Prophet, the Hand of God, so when I recognized my situation I now knew how to more than just "make it through." This time I knew I had help available. I asked for help and accepted that help. I listened and followed the Divine guidance given to me with love and compassion. I knew His comfort. I knew that even in the moments when I felt alone that I am never alone. Prophet is with me every moment. He helped me have the strength to do my part: to wisely use the tools and skills I had been taught in the past, and to truly know I could do it with him. So this time my experience with depression really was different, and I am forever grateful.

I kept praying for help and continued attending retreats at Guidance for a Better Life. That is where I originally learned about God's Prophet and the importance of our relationship. Everything continued to build toward a good outcome. The inner guide, the inner part of Prophet, and I spent time in scripture, reading spiritual books, putting love into everything we did throughout the day, and being grateful. Together we sang HU with my baby even in those tired, weary, early weeks and so much more. I paid attention to my dreams and used those late-night feedings awake with the baby as an opportunity to write them down and say, "Thank you." The Prophet nudged me to speak up for myself and take care of myself. He encouraged me to step out of my comfort zone and join activities and social groups where I met wonderful, welcoming people in the community.

God responded to my prayers by guiding and helping me daily. Life was enjoyable and not a struggle. I had faith in Him, and in turn He helped me have faith in myself to keep going forward. I came out better than ever, and feel I have a stronger and deeper relationship with Prophet than I even had before. My life was good, but now I was appreciating it more. My sacred relationship with Prophet makes my life abundant, and it is continually growing.

Instead of spiraling down and retreating into depression like I had in the past, I stepped out, survived, and then thrived with my focus on God's Love. Things were not distorted as they had been before in that same space and frame of mind because the Prophet helped me to see clearly from a higher view, as Soul. That higher view helped me to appreciate the gifts of God that were everywhere around me. My heart was open and filled with love, which gave me the opportunity to enjoy loving and caring for my family again. I allowed love in, so I could give it out to others, and was shown a deeper understanding of giving and receiving love. I am very thankful for the blessing to walk with Prophet daily and to give and receive God's Love. It has changed my life.

Written by Michelle Hibshman

Prayer to Find a Job

Many times our prayers are heard, and answered, but we miss taking the steps needed to make them a reality. The Divine will guide us in the direction to answer our prayers, but we will never get there if we cannot "hear" the guidance. It pays, literally — in the following story, to learn how to listen to those gentle whisperings.

I had a sincere prayer in my heart to find a new job and I expressed this in prayer to God. I realized it would not happen without some effort on my part, so I polished my resume and applied for a couple jobs in the area I was interested in living. After receiving some mild interest from one company, and some weeks passing by, I decided to apply to a few more positions. I got a call one Tuesday from a company requesting a one-hour phone interview. The company was located four hours from my home, but it just so happened I was going to be traveling to that area the upcoming weekend, so I was available for an on-site interview. To me an in-person interview was much better than a phone interview. The Divine was already helping! I have come to learn from Prophet that apparent "coincidences" are not just luck or by chance, rather they are blessings from the Divine. The timing to my interview was one such blessing.

After confirming a meeting time, I started preparing for the interview. I prayed to God for help and sang HU to get in tune with the Divine. What questions should I be prepared to answer? What questions do I ask of them? I researched the company and the position. I anticipated some of the questions that I might be asked, and I rehearsed my responses the best I could, but the possibilities were endless. All through this process I felt Del, the Prophet, guide me to very specific questions.

The morning of the interview I sang HU, invited Prophet to be with me, and surrendered the outcome. This was very comforting because I trusted the outcome would be perfect regardless if it resulted in a job offer or not. The hiring manager explained this was a time for them to get to know me and for me to learn if this was a position that interested me — this was precisely the insight I received during my preparation! As the interview progressed I was asked ten questions, and of the countless questions that could have been asked in an interview, I had rehearsed and prepared for every one of the ten. Prophet had prepared me for those exact questions, an answer to my prayer. The interview conversation flowed naturally, and everyone seemed to be at ease. This experience is one of many over the years that have confirmed my prayers are heard! God loves us and wants us to live happy and abundant lives, in all areas of life.

Written by Chris Hibshman

My Brother's Passing

Losing a loved one is hard enough. It can be even more challenging when they take their own life. Too often people fall into feeling guilty at what could have been done to prevent it. This is a losing battle, one that will close your heart and pull you down. We must accept that they are ultimately responsible for their decisions — the good ones and the bad ones. We must also have faith that God does indeed still love them and that they will not be eternally damned. Ask yourself if this is your idea of something a loving God would do, punish you forever for one mistake? Eternity is a long, long time. Would you cut off your child forever, withdrawing all love for one lapse in judgment? Are those that take their own life still loved by God — absolutely. Are they still held responsible — absolutely. And what does that look like? Most likely a quick return into a new body to begin again, usually into a similar situation where they have another chance to face the challenges they struggled with before. Life is about growing into greater capacities of wisdom and love and it takes time. Time that a loving God graciously gives us.

I received a call from my mother who was frantically repeating over and over, "We lost him; we lost him." My eldest brother had died. He struggled most of his adult life with bipolar episodes. Numerous bipolar episodes and other serious ups and downs took a toll on his marriage. After a divorce his life became more unstable, and his life seemed to be spiraling downwards. On his birthday we talked by phone; I was looking forward to having time with him in person at Thanksgiving. That time never came.

After starting a new job in another city he became extremely depressed and ended up at the mental health unit. On that fateful day my parents had gone to petition for his early release into their care, saying they could provide a safe environment for him. My dad had left the keys to the car by the phone, and when they were all napping, Dave got up and slipped out of the house. The car was his means to end his life.

My family was grief-stricken and my parents were full of guilt. I also wondered what I could have done differently, and I too started feeling guilt. In contemplation, connecting with the Prophet on the inner, I received very strong inner guidance not to allow my heart to fill with guilt. He assured me that anything I might have done would not have changed the outcome for Dave. I felt a release from guilty feelings shortly after my contemplation. Without the guilt I was more able to support and comfort my family.

Two weeks after Dave had passed I prepared for my early morning contemplation, singing HU and connecting with the Divine on the inner. Instantly I found myself at a favorite spot by the pond at the Guidance for a Better Life retreat center. Prophet was standing to my right, and my attention was drawn to the left by some movement. There was my brother Dave, looking like he had in his late twenties. He looked robust and healthy. I was very happy to see him. I introduced him to the Prophet but then realized Dave already knew Prophet because he had brought Dave to me. My gratitude was immense to be with my brother once again.

My mother and father continued to suffer deeply with grief and guilt. I always thought my dad would live to be at least one hundred years old. He now seemed to age rapidly and was rather miserable and somewhat bitter. A month after his ninetieth birthday he had a stroke and died. I did not have the opportunity to say goodbye. Six months went by, and one evening as I sat down to HU at bedtime, suddenly there was my dad in my inner vision! He looked much younger, glowing with good health. It struck me how happy he looked and totally at peace. I do not recall him looking that happy or peaceful, ever.

I am very grateful to the Divine for giving me these precious experiences with my brother and my dad. Both experiences helped to heal my heart from my loss. And even though my brother ended his own life, breaking spiritual law, I know God still loves him and will care for him.

Written by Jan Reid

A Wave of God's Love

Each and every one of us can be a point of light in our respective spheres. Our friends, family, and the countless others whose paths we cross in the course of our day can be lifted up in our presence. It is a conscious choice on our part to stay tuned in with Spirit and allow the Love of God to flow through us - wherever we are. What a wonderful way to serve.

Several years ago I stood in line at the grocery store. The store was so crowded that even the line for the Express Lane went halfway down an aisle. As I waited I silently sang HU, that glorious love song to God, as taught to me by Del Hall, my teacher and a true Prophet of God. As the line crawled forward a large man got in line directly behind me. He seemed quite agitated. He complained rather loudly about the long line, slamming his keys repeatedly against a shelf. I felt uncomfortable standing next to him. Others in line seemed to be trying to pretend he or they were somewhere else. His intensity was building and it seemed like sooner or later someone was going to be on the receiving end of his apparent frustration. I was pretty sure the clerk running the cash register in our lane was going to be that someone.

The line shuffled along awkwardly for several more minutes until finally I reached the conveyor belt near the register. The man behind me said, "Excuse me," abruptly shoving his items down next to me. He grumbled again about having to wait so long. If you've ever worked in retail or worked a cash register you know that a single individual can sometimes greatly affect your day, especially when you are tired. You might see a hundred people in a day, but one single customer can stand out as being exceptionally kind or unpleasant. Prophet has taught for years that we affect others with our words, thoughts, and actions. We cannot control whether or not we send out waves of energy that impact others (either negatively or positively), but we do have control over what kind of energy we send out. "What kind of waves do you want to make?" Del would often ask us.

I had managed to keep my heart open and continued to sing HU silently in the checkout line when I got the nudge to speak to the man. With a deep breath and silent trust in the Prophet I turned and said, "Not very fast today, are they?" — stating the incredibly obvious. Instead of agitating him further, my words instead seemed to calm him. He agreed with my obvious statement and added that it is never fast. The Express Lane is *always* slow in every grocery store he goes into. I made another agreeable comment and then a weird thing happened. We both laughed. It was like Spirit turned a release valve and let off a great deal of pressure. It was very tangible.

I turned back in line and after a few more moments finally reached the cashier. I turned to him again and jokingly said, "End of the line, finally, you almost made it!" He chuckled and said, "Yeah, NOW it's the Express Lane!" When I finished paying he said, "You take care now." I looked back and smiled as I heard the cashier ask him, "How are you today?" The man calmly responded, "I'm doing okay, thank you."

Spirit will not violate one's free will, and it was not my intention to change the man's mind or mood. Singing HU kept my heart open to God, and the Holy Spirit found an opening to gracefully diffuse an uncomfortable situation. I was blessed to see the Hand of God grace my everyday life. Perhaps the man was blessed to cast some of his cares behind and have a better day, and the cashier was spared from a potentially unpleasant interaction.

Life is full of situations like that, seemingly small and commonplace experiences that challenge and test us. These experiences offer the opportunity to be a victim of circumstances or remain above the fray. Being aware of Prophet spiritually as we go about our day can inspire us to be more of the cause in our lives and less the effect of others' moods, words, and opinions. How freeing this is to experience! God loves us and wants us to be happy! How incredibly blessed I am to know a living Prophet who teaches me to do this very thing. What kind of waves do you want to send out?

Written by Chris Comfort

The Light and Sound of God

There are beautiful examples in holy books of people experiencing the Light and Sound of God. Many can accept the truth in this, yet some have a hard time accepting that it still happens in this day and age. I can assure you that it does. God can shower His Light and Love on anyone, anytime. This in no way takes away from the service of those from the past. Instead, it glorifies and testifies to the continuing magnitude of a loving God who knows each and every one of us.

Many have heard of or read about the Light of God — God's Light. There are references of the Light of God in the Bible. One example is Jesus saying, "… I am the light of the world …" John 8:12 (KJV). Another example is about Saint Paul, then Saul, while traveling on the road to Damascus saw a light from Heaven, brighter than the sun, blazing around him and his companions. (Acts 26:13)

My first experience with the Light of God was during one of my first retreats as a student at Guidance for a Better Life, almost fifteen years ago. My teacher, a Prophet of God, was leading the class of many students in a guided contemplation. Together we sang HU, a love song to God. I could feel God's Love and Presence all around me. In the darkness of the unlit room, I began seeing beautiful swirling colors of blue light in front of me. I could see this beautiful blue light with my eyes open and with them closed. Then a blue light in the shape of a heart appeared before me. I felt God's Love with me and within me, Soul.

The next day Del gave the class the opportunity to share experiences from the guided contemplation. I shared my experience of the blue light and the blue heart. Del explained that the blue light and blue heart are a calling card of the Prophet who was letting me know that he loves me and is always with me. My heart filled with love, joy, and deep appreciation for this gift of love from God! Throughout the years as a student at the retreat center, I have been blessed with numerous experiences and blessings with the Light of God. Sometimes the light is blue, sometimes golden, and sometimes a brilliant white light.

I have also been blessed with the gift from the Divine of learning about the Sound of God — God's Voice. I am so blessed to have had many experiences with the Sound of God. The Sound or Voice of God is in everything, as is the Light of God. Everything and everyone — every Soul — is made of the Light and Sound of God. It is the Divine Spirit of God. It is also known as the Holy Ghost or the Holy Spirit, and other names. It is the life force from God, which can be seen and heard with our spiritual eyes and ears, and even with our physical eyes and ears, when we have the awareness to see and hear them. In the Bible there are references to the Sound of God. One is at Pentecost when the Apostles were all together in one place "And suddenly there came a sound from heaven as of a rushing mighty wind, and it filled all the house where they were sitting." Acts 2:2 (KJV)

I am blessed to have heard the Sound, the Voice of God in many forms, with both my spiritual and physical ears. Often when singing HU at a retreat at the school, or at home, I hear the Sound of God as music. Music "not of this world." Music of the Spheres. It is a music unlike any type or genre of music of this Earth, a sound impossible to reproduce with any musical instrument or singer's voice, and difficult if not impossible to describe or explain in words. It is a sound I hear only while I am singing HU. As a musician, I know that hearing this special music is a very personal gift of God's Love to me.

While singing HU sometimes I hear the Voice of God as sounds of low, warm, soothing tones. While I cannot hear or decipher actual words, when I hear it I am filled with love, peace, joy, and comfort — all beautiful gifts of God's Love.

I am so very appreciative of and grateful to the Prophet for these amazing gifts of the Light and Sound of God, these gifts of love, and for the blessing of having the eyes and ears to see and hear them. I am so grateful for the HU.

Written by Cathy Sandman

Creator Please "Show Me Love"

"Can you accept that you have seen the Light of God?" was the question posed to the author of this piece. What if this was your experience, could you accept a blessing of this nature?

It was dusk as I sat upon a small log beside the pond. Nightfall was gently rolling in upon this evening in the mountains. The setting was at a spiritual retreat at Guidance for a Better Life about twenty years ago. My spiritual teacher Del had prepared our class to participate in a spiritual exercise called "Show Me Love." Each student found a "sit area" somewhere near the pond. It was a time to slow down the inner and outer pace for an opportunity to invite Divine Spirit more consciously into our hearts. This was a new experience for me back then. We were asked to approach this spiritual exercise with the attitude of not expecting anything, yet being open and receptive to whatever Divine Spirit may want to show us. To help us relax it was suggested to look at the landscape using wide-angle vision. It is a technique that uses all of your senses to help one become more aware of your surroundings. Sitting quite still I could see the sand beach, the pond, willows, birds, bats catching insects, a small patch of buttercup flowers, and dusk becoming nightfall. Bullfrogs sang and there was a soft breeze. Now relaxed I began to sing HU. Del taught us the HU song, an ancient name for God. It is the most pure prayer known. It is sung without expecting anything in return from the Creator. It is simply a way to say I love you. I sang HU for what seemed five to ten minutes. Then I prayed, "Creator please show me love," sitting quietly with eyes closed learning to listen with my heart.

Very soon I began to smell the most fragrant scent of flowers. I had chosen the log to sit upon because of the buttercups that were beside it. As a child I admired the buttercup, yet knew it did not have such a large fragrance. I peeked at the buttercups, and then resumed the spiritual exercise. Next

I began to hear people talking and walking past me in conversation. I thought they did not hear our teacher say to respect everyone's space during this time. We would have time after the exercise to share our experiences. I peeked to see who was talking and no one was anywhere near. Slightly confused I sat quietly with eyes closed and continued to pray, "Creator please show me love." Once again I was disturbed by what seemed to be spotlights that were shining upon me. I opened my eyes and saw where the light was coming from. There appeared to be two huge round spotlights uphill from the pond beside Del and Lynne's home. They lit up the entire area with white light as though it was daytime. The lights seemed to be suspended in air as though on a wire moving gently up and down from a breeze. One was slightly larger than the other, appearing at least three feet wide. The light diffused around their circumferences. I was so puzzled by the lights being turned on and people talking during the spiritual exercise, that I opted to share only about the scent of flowers when we gathered afterwards to discuss our individual experiences. I did not want to insult others for what I thought at the time to be disruptions to the spiritual exercise.

Class was over for the evening, and I had a strong nudge to walk up the hill to the house and find those spotlights. While searching the area Del arrived on silent feet and said, "Who's there?" I replied, "It's me, Ann. I'm looking for the spotlights that someone turned on during the "Show Me Love" exercise. Del said quite clearly that they did not have any spotlights and asked, "Can you accept that you have seen the Light of God?" His words were a shocking contrast to my assumptions. His words left me speechless as he continued on into his home. My innate trust for Del allowed me to consider his question regarding my experiences. In time I was able to accept the realization and blessings received during the "Show Me Love" exercise that night. The Creator showed me spiritual light, spiritual sound, and spiritual scent! They were very clear ways of God showing me love. I needed time to grow into those realizations.

It is precious and necessary to have a spiritual teacher who understands the ways of Divine Spirit. Del taught me how to have and to understand my experience with the Light and Sound of God (the Holy Spirit). Then my world began to open up. I have grown to know that Divine Spirit communicates directly to all Souls. I am blessed to have been offered the spiritual tools to experience God's Love so directly. Knowing spiritual truths from experience has brought me a deep peace of heart. This peace is with me always.

When the Light of God visits in any form, be it lighting up the night or a tiny flash of light, it is a privilege to be conscious that Divine Spirit is communicating with me. Lighting up the night was, in part, a way to help me break through learned beliefs that the Light of God speaks only to those who wear religious robes or saints from the past. To grow in communication with Divine Spirit, heart-to-heart, is the great blessing of life.

Written by Ann Atwell

Thankful I Shared

The greatest hindrance to accepting our initial experiences with the Light and Sound of God can sometimes be ourselves. We let our mind, which is fearful of change, cause us to doubt. It is during times like these when it is key to have a teacher who understands the "Language of the Divine."

During my first three-day spiritual retreat at Guidance for a Better Life, Del encouraged us to participate in a relaxing sit exercise. During this sit exercise we were instructed to go find a place to sit outside, relax, and enjoy being in the mountains. I found a spot in the woods on a large smooth rock. After I got comfortable, I began to think of something I was grateful for to help open my heart. I then sang HU for a while. When I was done singing HU, I asked the Prophet to show me Divine Love. I looked around at my lush green oasis in the woods. I felt a wave of peace wash over me. I felt myself melt into the rock as I listened to the flowing stream rush by, the birds chirping around me, and the occasional call of a bullfrog. Directly in front of my field of vision was a twinkling orange light. I began to sing "Prophet" silently to myself several times. As I was singing "Prophet," I heard bells ringing. Soon after this, the sit exercise came to an end.

I went back up to the school for class. As time passed before I shared the experience with the group, I began to mentally talk myself out of the experience. I began to physically justify the light that I saw as spotlights mounted outside of the school that someone must have happened to turn on. Since this was my first spiritual class at the retreat center, I thought that I was too new at this to experience the Divine Light of God. Boy was I wrong!

I felt multiple nudges from the inner Prophet that I should share my experience with the group. Since I was not sure if I had actually experienced something, I felt a good bit of hesitancy. After hearing many other individuals share their experiences during the exercise, I finally decided to share my experience with the group. When I shared, I received so much clarity on my experience. I learned that I was actually at the second Heaven during my experience. I knew I was at this Heaven because of the color orange and the tinkling of bells. These colors and sounds I thought I had made up or misconstrued as physical light were actually God responding to me! By opening my heart and singing a love song to God, God responded by telling me that "I am loved by God." Had I not shared this experience with Del, I may have easily talked myself out of this Divine blessing, this gift of love from God. I may have missed that God not only heard me, but responded to me. The purpose of this exercise was to have the Prophet show us Divine Love. Sometimes this response from God may be so subtle that we are not even aware of it. Thank you Prophet for nudging me to share with the class, otherwise I may have totally missed this Divine gift of love from God!

Written by Michelle Reuschling

I Heard Heavenly Music

Within the Heavenly realms the Voice of God, or the Holy Spirit, manifests itself in a wide range of spiritual light and sound. Often the color of the light, or in the following case the sound heard, is a road map of sorts to which Heavenly plane Soul is on. God delivers His Love to Soul via the light and sound, so to experience the Voice of God in any form is a profound blessing.

Throughout my spiritual studies I had oftentimes read about the beautiful sounds that can be heard on the various spiritual planes of existence. In my heart I desired that I might have an experience of hearing Heavenly music, but it was not forthcoming until just recently. On June 7, 2015 many gathered in singing HU, a love song to God, in the presence of Prophet Del Hall. I began by letting go of all external distractions. I prayed to become a perfect vehicle for God's Love, all the while opening my heart to allow a continuous stream of God's Love to flow through it with each wave of HU.

There was a sense of being lifted up spiritually higher as we continued to send love out to the unseen worlds. We had been singing for about ten minutes when, within the sound of those singing HU, I distinctly heard the sound of a flute. Elated about the blessing of hearing the sound of the fifth Heaven, the Soul Plane, my heart soared with love as I sang to my Heavenly Father. More sound came into my awareness; it was of violins, the sound that originates on the eighth Heaven. I now had personally been blessed to experience the Holy Spirit, God's Voice, as both Light and Sound!

I was allowed to experience these sounds in order that I might testify to the reality of Soul's ability to travel in worlds beyond what the physical eyes can see. I also know that to experience God's Light or Sound is a special gift of love. Since I was singing in the presence of the Prophet of God, there was a plus factor at play that one will only know by direct experience.

In appreciation of and gratitude for the blessings!   Written by Bernadette Spitale

An Ancient Name of God

When you express your love and gratitude to God by singing HU, it is received; you are most certainly heard. Deeper realizations and insights on the profound blessing of HU will continue to grow every year for those who sing it.

Each spring the students of Guidance for a Better Life and their families come together for a Spring Clean-up Weekend to help prepare the retreat center for the coming year. On the surface it looks like work, but really it is sheer joy. Traditionally the weekend includes a bountiful potluck dinner Saturday evening and a family HU Sing Sunday morning.

This year we gathered in the Beach House on Sunday morning as in years past. My view from where I was seated at the back of the room allowed me to see all the families together and the excitement and smiles of the children. I love hearing their beautiful voices, and it is a treat having them join us. Prophet

Del Hall began by reviewing and explaining that HU is both a love song to God and an ancient name for God, and when we sing it we are essentially calling His name. He reminded us to be fully present in the moment when singing HU, to put love into how we sing, paying attention to how we form the word and enunciate the sound, and to do our best to sing in a pleasant, natural tone that blends harmoniously with others. In this way we demonstrate love and reverence to God.

Prophet then did something I will never forget to emphasize the profound sacredness of singing HU. He did a kind of role-play, acting out what it might be like as God hears us calling to Him by singing His name. In a light-hearted but purposeful way, he turned away from us and pretended to be God busy at whatever He might be doing. When God hears someone singing His name and calling to Him he turns to them and asks, "Yes my child, what can I do for you?" Prophet turned and looked directly at us as he said these words, but he was no longer play-acting; it was real. Physically I was in the last row of a room full of people when he did this, but my inner experience was as if I was the only one in the room. I was up very close to him, face-to-face, and God was looking right at me through the eyes of Prophet. In His Eyes was eternity. An endless well of Divine love poured out, seared through me, knew me, and melted my heart. Love poured out of me back to Him. In an instant I was nurtured, loved, comforted, reassured, strengthened, and personally recognized by Almighty God, my Heavenly Father. My heart was so full, and I felt more tender and softened as I sang this beautiful love song and ancient name of God, carefully forming and savoring every precious HU I sang to Him.

This experience has sweetened and renewed every HU since. I remember how it felt to be held in that gaze of Divine love. I re-experience how that love tenderized my heart and brought forth an even greater love and appreciation to express back. Singing HU was an incredibly beautiful prayer before this, and now it is even more beautiful, more personal, and more sacred. I feel closer to my Heavenly

Father, and though I know He hears every HU, every prayer, somehow this experience has made this knowing exist at an even deeper level and be even more real. Prophet taught me about HU over twenty years ago. In the time since he has revealed some of its profound blessings and has given layer upon layer of experiences, understanding, and insights, and yet there is still more to learn, as I experienced here.

What happened this day also shows that, as a Prophet of God, Del can be teaching in a room full of people and be working with each one of his students individually on a very personal level. It gives one a glimpse into the Divine nature of Prophet and one of his many aspects, the Voice of God. He also provides a perfectly clear channel for God to reach out to us. What I experienced is really what Prophet's mission is all about: to take down walls and remove barriers between God and His children, to strengthen our communication and love connection with God, and to bring us closer together with our Father in Heaven.

Written by Lorraine Fortier

Bathed and Showered in God's Love

God's Light and Love pour into this world. There is no limit to it other than our ability to accept it. God is always aware of our level of receptiveness and when He sees an opportunity to shower us with more of His Love He does not hesitate.

Down here in the physical, we are constantly being bombarded with negative, it's all around us. It depletes and drains us of our light and our love and can slowly create a wedge between us and our Heavenly Father. So, God in His wisdom, has sent us His Prophet to help us find our way back home. There is always a God-chosen representative on the physical planet. This is one of those incredible gifts I was blessed with during a HU sing contemplation with Del.

The lights in the room were turned down low, we sat silently for a moment, I stilled my thoughts. Del asked us to gently focus on our breathing. I sat quietly relaxing and slowly breathed in and out. For the next fifteen to twenty minutes, we sang HU rhythmically over and over, sending our love to God, asking for nothing in return. As I did, I gradually felt my breathing aligning with something greater than myself. I could now feel a deeper sense of Divine peace and calm start to grow within. It seems to be part of God's nature to bless us with gifts of His Love whenever He sees an opportunity that we are open, receptive, and will accept it. Today was one of those windows.

I became aware of the inner worlds, the Heavenly worlds. Del then escorted us to a spiritual Temple of God and we walked into the Light. I now stood with Prophet in a beautiful white beam of light and was engulfed by the magnificent heavenly Sound of the HU. It was all encompassing, all that existed, I was being bathed within the Light and Sound, the Voice of God, the Holy Spirit, the Love of God. I was being saturated, cleansed in a purifying shower of Light that helped to remove the accumulated crud that seems to coat everything down here in the physical. This beam was filled with and filled me with God's Love, peace, joy, clarity, and Grace.

Slowly, I saw the color transformed from a beautiful white light to a sparkling gold. At first, I was aware of one small drop of this golden Love from God and then another and another until it filled my total awareness as a gentle rain. We have experienced over the years that one small drop of God's Love would be enough to nourish, sustain, heal, purify, everything, yet God in all His magnificence blesses us with His Love when there is a window of opportunity when we are receptive. Because of Prophet and the HU I was receptive. We were now being bathed and showered in a continuous downpour of God's golden Love. I accepted and drank in all I could.

This golden light washed and fortified my entire being both spiritually and physically. It cleansed and removed everything negative, unwanted, and useless and filled and replaced it with His Divine Light. God's Love! I sat and savored this moment as long as I could. I slowly returned back to conscious awareness of the physical room and I was grateful and blessed beyond what I have words to convey.

Written by Jason Levinson

I Held Her in Heaven

We all as Soul live many, many lifetimes. During our earthly incarnations we develop love connections with other Souls, and often we are blessed to reincarnate with the same Souls to continue our journey together. The following is a beautiful story of a mother-to-be meeting her future daughter in the inner spiritual worlds.

I have a daughter who is nearly two and a half years old. My pregnancy with her almost seems like a dream now. I can recall snippets, but mostly I remember the wondering and the waiting. A lot of that goes on in nine months. "What will she be like? Will we get along?" As first-time parents my husband and I really had no clue what to expect. While much of this time is fading from memory there is one experience I had while pregnant I will never forget. It has forever changed the way I see my daughter, and the way I view our family. Prophet allowed me to meet and hold my daughter, before she was born, in Heaven.

I was five months pregnant while at a retreat at Guidance for a Better Life. This is one of my favorite places to be. As a group we sang HU and focused on sending our love and gratitude to God. In the quietude after singing HU I left my body spiritually, as Soul, and Prophet took me to Heaven, our true Home. Each journey to this sacred place has been different. Each visit has helped me, degree by degree, to understand the tremendous love God has for me personally and for all of His Creation.

This time, I knelt with Prophet at the edge of God's Ocean. It was night and the water was calm. It was a gift of love from God to see it this way because there is a special beauty to me about the physical ocean at nighttime. I could feel the presence of God's Love and peace all around me and in me. I savored being in the moment experiencing the quiet stillness, like being held in a loving embrace.

Just being allowed to be here was a most incredible thing, and yet Prophet gave me another personal and sacred blessing. I looked out across the water to see a beautiful being of light emerge from the velvety depths of God's Ocean. This being was in a female form. As the being came closer I saw she was carrying something, and to my surprise it was the Soul that would be my future daughter, Camille. The beautiful being stood in front of me holding this precious Soul in her arms, as one would cradle a cherished baby. Camille was made of God's Light and Sound. The way she moved in this being's arms was the same as in my womb, as though bursting to get out, a literal bundle of joy.

The being of light silently handed Camille to me with care, and I was allowed to hold her for a moment. It did not feel like my daughter and I were meeting for the first time. It was more a reunion of two Souls happy to see each other once again. I loved her and she loved me. How incredible to know the Soul being born into my family was indeed a Soul I had known and loved before. I was speechless. To be here in Heaven was amazing in itself, but I was also being reunited with a Soul that was to be my future daughter. Now I was even more excited and could not wait for her to be born. I could not wait for the moment when she, Soul, would animate her physical body; the moment when she would take her first breath of life in this world, and I could kiss her sweet face.

Then I gave her back to the being of light who returned into God's Ocean. I was filled with wonder and appreciation that God allowed us to meet in this sacred place. Soul, being eternal, is ageless, yet I was allowed to meet her in the form she would be taking in her new physical embodiment, that of my daughter. In this way I could hold her as I was so longing to do. This was a stunning gift from God.

Being allowed to meet my daughter before she was born into this life taught me more about the remarkable love God has for each Soul. I learned that Soul is a child of God whose true Home is in Heaven. Our sons and daughters are not randomly selected but are given to us with purpose by God's loving design. It does not matter if we are born into a family or adopted. Our families are part of a love story that started before this lifetime and will continue into future lives. In His timing God will reconnect us with our loved ones again.

I am so grateful Camille joined our family, and I can love her again. She is such a delight! I look forward to the day when I can share with her the story of how I held her in Heaven.

Written by Carmen Snodgrass

In Our Father's Eyes

This is an amazing testimony on visiting the Abode of God. Traveling spiritually in full consciousness to the source of all — to the Home of Our Father. Guided there by the Prophet to receive healing, revelation, comfort, and a profound insight — we are each loved unconditionally by God. Being able to accept this love changes everything.

Do you know we are welcome in Heaven? Do you know God loves you no matter what you are facing in life? Out of the many, many blessings that being a student of Del's has given me, this following experience stands out as one that gave me an understanding that God's Love for us truly has no conditions. Knowing this has given me a peace that has changed how I walk through life.

Some years ago, I was going through a time where I was struggling with jealousy and envy. I was not comfortable in my own skin, and thought if I was more like someone else or had what they had in their lives, then I would be happy. While logically I knew that this was unhealthy, I could not seem to shake it. In my eyes, I was not deserving of love.

During a weeklong spiritual retreat at Guidance for a Better Life Del led us in singing HU. After some time, I became aware I was in front of a huge ocean made entirely of God's Love. Instinctively, I knelt. I was not alone, Prophet was next to me holding my hand. Beside me were Souls as far as I could see. Each one of us was made of glowing, shimmering light. Each one of us was beautiful. We were each kneeling along this beach in love and reverence to our Heavenly Father. As I looked out over the wide expanse, I saw pure white light reflecting in the distant water. The light came closer to me, and I saw a form appear sitting in a gigantic chair. The Heavenly Father was seated before us. I could see and feel our love going out to Him with each HU and then returning back to us in a beautiful rhythm.

As I was kneeling before this immense ocean of God's Love, I was experiencing such a deep, deep peace. I have never experienced this much peace in my life. I needed nothing and I lacked nothing. Peace filled every fiber of my being. Tears streamed down my face as I accepted the love that was being offered to me. Then, our Heavenly Father arose and came towards me across the water. With such a gentleness He lifted my head and kissed my forehead. "I love you and I am glad you are here." His Eyes filled the sky, immense and loving. His Love continued to pour into me, filling every part of me.

I knew then, as I do now, that He loves me without conditions. He has the same love for you, no matter what you are struggling with inside or going through in life. Our Father truly loves us unconditionally and accepting this love truly changes us.

For days, and now years later, I close my eyes and return to this living experience of God's Love. Seeing the love in my Heavenly Father's Eyes, face-to-face, gave me a confidence in His Love for me that is unshakable. Thank you Prophet for guiding me home to Heaven to meet our Father, face-to-face.   Written by Molly Comfort

God Touched My Heart

You are loved by God, and one of His desires is for you to know and live in this love daily. With the Prophet as your guide you can spiritually travel into the Heavens and experience this love from an aspect of the Divine for yourself — before the end of this physical life. Many who have been blessed to experience God's Love directly have one thing in common — they desire for you to experience it as well.

It was while I was deep in contemplation that I was blessed with an amazing experience of God's Love. It was given to me after singing HU, an ancient name for God, for a good length of time. As I sat with my physical eyes closed, my attention on the inner reality within me, I was aware of my spiritual teacher whom I know as the Prophet, right beside me. He guided the real eternal me, Soul, higher and higher through world upon world of God's Creation, the house of many mansions Jesus spoke of two thousand years ago. Prophet took me all the way home to the Abode of God Himself. I can best describe it as an expanse of God's Love and Mercy, one so vast it was like a boundless ocean.

To be allowed to consciously return to my true Home where God created me as Soul was a profound gift in and of itself. Yet God always has more love to give, for amid the ocean waves of God's Love, there appeared the Lord Himself in a form I could relate to, one more personal than the boundless ocean. The Lord placed His Hand on my heart and held it there. His eternal Love poured into me, and I knew beyond any shadow of a doubt that God truly loves me, and has always loved me. Without conditions and without judgments He loves me. It is a love that has no beginning and no end. During that moment I knew His Love is eternal and that it is personal, for God knows me and loves me just as much as any other part of His Creation, and He loves me just as I am. I did not earn this gift, but I was blessed to be able to receive it by the Grace of the Lord.

In the years since this Divine blessing of blessings there have been many times when I have not felt as loved as I did during that moment in eternity. Love is more than a feeling though, for when I remember this blessing of standing before God as He touched me, I know that whether or not I feel loved, God loves me, and that all is well as I walk in His Love. This gift of God touching my heart, for which I thank the Prophet, the one whom God has ordained to take Soul home to Him, is a blessing that was not given to me just for my own benefit, or to be hoarded selfishly like a prized possession.

This gift of Divine love has blessed me with a greater capacity to give and receive love. It has helped to liberate me from selfish desires, to think more of the needs of others, and to truly hear and know in my heart what God, through His Prophet, is asking me to do. I also know that the love was given to me so I can testify to this: God is real and God loves you.

Written by Roland Vonder Muhll

Guidance for a Better Life
Our Story

My Father's Journey

God always has a living Prophet on Earth to teach His ways and accomplish His will. My father, Del Hall III, is currently God's true Prophet fully raised up and ordained by God Himself. He was not always a Prophet, nor did he even know what a Prophet

Prophet Del Hall III

was, but God had a plan for him like He has for all of His children. Over many years through many life experiences, God had begun to prepare my father for his future assignment, mostly unbeknownst to him. Everything he experienced in his life from the joys to the sadness helped prepare him for his future role as Prophet.

My dad grew up in California and was a decent student but a better athlete. He received an appointment to the United States Naval Academy in Annapolis, Maryland where he later met my mother. They were married two days after he graduated and received his commission as an officer. After a short tour on a Navy ship deployed to Vietnam, he went to flight training school and became a Navy fighter pilot. While attending flight school in Pensacola, Florida he also earned a Master of Science Degree and had the first of his three children, a son. After flight school he was stationed in a fighter squadron on the east coast, where he and my mom began investing in real estate, adding to their family with the birth of two daughters. Following this tour of duty he was assigned as a jet flight instructor in Texas, after which, his time in the Navy was finished. He was a natural pilot and loved his time in the sky, but it was time to move on.

So far in life he had no real concern for, or even thought much about God, religion, or spiritual matters in general. He lived life fully. He raised his family. He traveled. He invested and became an entrepreneur starting and growing highly successful businesses in diverse fields ranging from real estate to aerospace consulting. Years before however, a seed had been planted when God's eternal teachings were introduced to him in his late teens, and while it did not show outwardly, the truth in these teachings spoke to his heart. My dad might not have been giving much thought to God up to this point in his life, but God was definitely thinking about him and the future He had planned for him. Like an acorn destined to become a mighty oak, the seed that lay dormant in his heart would someday be stirred to life. Through all his life experiences, both "good" and "bad," God would be preparing him for his future role as His Prophet.

When God decided it was time, He called my dad to Him. He did this by shutting down the world of financial security my dad had built. Over a period of two years all of his businesses were wound down and dissolved. What seemed like security turned out to be an illusion. Financial success had not provided true security. He now had failed businesses and a failing marriage and was trying to fix things without God's help, principles, or guidance. As painful as this time in his life was, it was yet another step towards the glorious life of service awaiting my father. God was removing him from the world my dad had created and furthering him along his path to his future role as Prophet.

After his marriage ended and his businesses wound down, he started fresh by going out west to give flying lessons near Lake Mead, Nevada. While living in Nevada my dad was reintroduced to the eternal teachings of God he first learned of as a teenager twenty-three years earlier, and though they resonated with him at the time, his priorities were different back then. Now, his serious training could begin. He started having very clear experiences with the Holy Spirit and noticed there was a familiarity with these teachings and experiences. He embraced the long hours of instruction, which often lasted until sunrise, and was receptive to the personal spiritual experiences he was given. This began an intense period of study and desire for spiritual truth that continues to this day. Some of his most profound and meaningful experiences during this time were with past Prophets of old. They came to him spiritually in contemplations and dreams. He learned of their roles in history and how they were raised up and ordained by God directly. He began to realize they were training him but was not clear why. A few times his experiences led him to believe he was in training to be a future Prophet. However, that revelation made no sense to him because he felt he was an imperfect person who made mistakes and had failures. He thought of the past and current Prophets of God as perfected Souls, not imperfect like he felt he was. Why would God choose him for such a role? He did not feel qualified.

Besides being introduced to God's teachings while he was out west, my father was blessed to meet his current wife Lynne. Returning to the East Coast, my father and Lynne moved into a small cabin on land he had acquired before his businesses shut down. This was a major change in his life, but it felt deeply right within him. He began to remember a desire to live like this as a child; from early childhood my dad found clarity and peace in nature. He had forgotten about this until now, but God had not and made this dream a reality. In addition to being their home, these beautiful, three-hundred-plus acres of land in the Blue Ridge Mountains would eventually become the location for the Guidance for a Better Life retreat center. The perfection of my father's experiences from earlier in his life in real estate, providing the land for his next step in life, speak to the perfection of God's plan. One of many, many examples I could list.

For many years my dad took wilderness skills courses around the country. He specialized in the study of wild edible and medicinal plants, tracking, and awareness skills, and authored articles for publication. Inspired to help folks feel more comfortable in the outdoors, my dad and Lynne began the Nature Awareness School in 1990. Classes were focused on teaching awareness and the primitive living skills needed to enjoy the woods and survive in them if necessary. An amazing thing happened within those first few years though; students began to experience aspects of God in very personal and dramatic ways. Somewhat like my dad's experience out west, they found that stepping away from their daily routine and the hustle of life, if even for a few days, created space for Spirit to do Its work. Whether they were enjoying the beauty of the Virginia wilderness and tranquility of the school grounds or relaxing by the pond, he found students' hearts opened, and they became more receptive to the Divine Hand that is always reaching out to Its children. More and more the discourse during wilderness classes shifted to the meanings of dreams, personal growth, finding balance in life, and experiences the students were having with the Voice of God in Its many forms. An increase of spiritual retreats was offered to fulfill the demand and over time became the predominant class offerings; the wilderness survival skills classes eventually fading away completely. The name "Nature Awareness School" seemed to be less fitting for what was actually being taught now and in February 2019 my father changed the name of the retreat center to Guidance for a Better Life.

Throughout this time my father's training and spiritual study continued. My father reached mastership and was ordained by God on July 7, 1999 but he was still not yet Prophet, more was required. On October 22, 2012, twenty-five years since his full-time intensive training had begun, God ordained him as His chosen Prophet, and He has continued to raise him up further since. God works through my father in very direct and beneficial ways for his students. Hundreds and hundreds of students over the past thirty years have received God's eternal teachings through my father's instruction and mentoring. They have had personal experiences with the Divine which have transformed and greatly blessed their lives. My father's greatest joy is being used by God as a servant to share God's ways and truths with thirsty Souls and hungry seekers. In addition to mountaintop retreats, my father continues to spread God's ways and teachings that so greatly blessed his life and the lives of his loved ones in many ways.

The book you hold in your hand is but one of more than a dozen titles we have co-authored. These incredible testimonies of God's Love are being shared in print, eBook, audio, YouTube videos and podcasts in hopes of blessing others.

Maybe you are at a turning point in your life and looking for direction. Maybe you have a knowing there is more to life but not sure what that might be or how to find it. Or, maybe you are simply drawn to what you read and hear in our stories. God speaks to our hearts and calls each of us in many different ways. Like my father's journey demonstrates, it doesn't matter where you started or the twists, turns, or seeming dead ends your life has taken; God wants us to know Him more fully, and for us to know our purpose within His Creation. He wants us to experience His Love regardless of our religious path or lack thereof. He always has a living Prophet here on Earth to help us accomplish His desire for us — to show us the way home to Him and to experience more abundance in our life while we are still living here on Earth. God's Prophet today is my father, Del Hall III. You have the opportunity to grow spiritually through God's teachings which Prophet shares. His guidance for a better life is available for you — please accept it.

Written by Del Hall IV

My Son, Del Hall IV

My son, Del Hall IV, joined Guidance for a Better Life as an instructor after fifteen years of in-class training with me, his father. He helped develop the five step "Keys to Spiritual Freedom" study

Del Hall IV

program and facilitates the first two courses in the program: Step One "Tools for Divine Guidance" and Step Two "Understanding Divine Guidance." Del also teaches people about the rich history of dream study and how to better recall their own dreams during the "Dream Study Workshops," which he hosts around the country. He is qualified to stepin and facilitate any of my retreats should the need arise.

Del is also Vice President of Marketing and helps with everything required to get the "good news" from Guidance for a Better Life out to hungry seekers: everything from book publishing, blogging, podcasts, and other social media outlets. He is co-author and book cover designer for many of our, thus far, fourteen published books.

My son loves the opportunity to work on creative projects for Guidance for a Better Life. From a very early age he has been an artist and loved creating artwork in multiple mediums. He was accepted into gifted art programs in Virginia Beach and then after high school graduation he attended the School of the Museum of Fine Arts in Boston. He is now a nationally exhibited artist and his paintings of the Light and Sound of God are in over seventy-five public and private collections. One of the greatest joys of the painting process for Del is using his paintings as an opportunity to share with others the inspiration behind them, God's Love and his experiences with the Light and Sound of God, the Holy Spirit, in contemplation and in waking life.

Del lives on the retreat center property in the Blue Ridge Mountains of Virginia with his wife and my three grandchildren whom they homeschool. He loves woodworking, tending to his vegetable garden, pruning his fruit trees, and helping maintain the beautiful three-hundred acres of retreat center property for students to enjoy. There is always something that needs attention on the land and Del is always up to the challenge. He loves to travel and spends his free time enjoying this beautiful country with his family in their RV.

My son has had multiple brain surgeries starting when he was seventeen years old for a recurring brain tumor. He credits God for surviving and thriving all this time when most with his condition do not. He looks to the sunrise every day with gratitude for yet another chance at life. With that chance he desires to help me share the love and teachings of God that have so blessed our lives. I pray to God daily thanking Him for my son's good health.

Written by Prophet Del Hall III

What is the Role of God's Prophet?

An introductory understanding of God's handpicked and Divinely trained Prophet is necessary to fully benefit from reading this book. God ALWAYS has a living Prophet of His choice on Earth. He has a physical body with a limited number of students, but the inner spiritual side of Prophet is limitless. Spiritually he can help countless numbers of Souls all over the world, no matter what religion or path they are on — even if that is no path at all. He teaches the ways of God and shares the Light and Sound of God. He delivers the living Word of God. Prophet can teach you physically as well as through dreams, and he can lift you into the Heavens of God. He offers protection, peace, teachings, guidance, healing, and love.

Each of God's Prophets throughout history has a unique mission. One may only have a few students with the sole intent to keep

God's teachings and truth alive. God may use another to change the course of history. God's Prophets are usually trained by both the current and former Prophets. The Prophet is tested and trained over a very long period of time. The earlier Prophets are physically gone but teach the new Prophet in the inner spiritual worlds. This serves two main purposes: the trainee becomes very adept at spiritual travel and gains wisdom from those in whose shoes he will someday walk. This is vital training because the Prophet is the one who must safely prepare and then take his students into the Heavens and back.

There are many levels of Heaven, also called planes or mansions. Saint Paul once claimed to know a man who went to the third Heaven. Actually it was Paul himself that went, but the pearl is, if there is a third Heaven, it presumes a first and second Heaven also exist. The first Heaven is often referred to as the Astral Plane. Even on just that one plane of existence there are over one hundred sub-planes. This Heaven is where most people go after passing, unless they receive training while still here in their physical body. Without a guide who is trained properly in the ways of God a student could misunderstand the intended lesson and become confused as to what is truth. The inner worlds are enormous compared to the physical worlds. They are very real and can be explored safely when guided by God's Prophet.

Part of my mission is to share more of what is spiritually possible for you as a child of God. Few Souls know or understand that God's Prophet can safely guide God's children, while still alive physically, to their Heavenly Home. Taking a child of God into the Heavens is not the job of clergy. Clergy have a responsibility to pass on the teaching of their religion exactly as they were taught, not to add additional concepts or possibilities. If every clergy member taught their own personal belief system no religion could survive for long. Then the beautiful teachings of an earlier Prophet of God would be lost. Clergy can be creative in finding interesting and uplifting ways to share their teachings, but their job is to keep their religion intact.

However, God sends His Prophets to build on the teachings of His past Prophets, to share God's Light and Love, to teach His language, and to guide Souls to their Heavenly Home.

There is ALWAYS MORE when it comes to God's teachings and truth. No one Prophet can teach ALL of God's ways. It may be that the audience of a particular time in history cannot absorb more wisdom. It could be due to a Prophet's limited time to teach and limited time in a physical body on Earth. Ultimately, it is that there is ALWAYS MORE! Each of God's Prophets brings additional teachings and opportunities for ways to draw closer to God, building on the work and teachings of former Prophets. That is one reason why Prophets of the past ask God to send another; to comfort, teach, and continue to help God's children grow into greater abundance. Former Prophets continue to have great love for God's children and want to see them continue to grow in accepting more of God's Love. One never needs to stop loving or accepting help from a past Prophet in order to grow with the help of the current Prophet.

All true Prophets of God work together and help one another to do God's work.

All the testimonies in this book were written by students at the Guidance for a Better Life retreat center. It is here that the nature of God, the Holy Spirit, and the nature of Soul are EXPERIENCED under the guidance of a true living Prophet of God. Guidance for a Better Life is NOT a religion, it is a retreat center. God and His Prophet are NOT disparaging of any religion of love. However, the more a path defines itself with its teachings, dogma, or tenets, the more "walls" it inadvertently creates between the seeker and God. Sometimes it even puts God into a smaller box. God does not fit in any box. Prophet is for all Souls and is purposely not officially aligned with any path, but shows respect to all.

YOU can truly have an ABUNDANT LIFE through a personal and loving relationship with God, the Holy Spirit, and God's ordained Prophet. This is my primary message to you. Having a closer relationship with the Divine requires understanding the "Language of the

Divine." God expresses His Love to us, His children, in many different and sometimes very subtle ways. Often His Love goes unrecognized and unaccepted because His language is not well known. The testimonies in this book have shown you some of the ways in which God expresses His Love. It is my hope that in reading this book, you have begun to learn more of the "Language of the Divine." The stories span from very subtle Divine guidance to profound examples of experiencing God up close and very personal. After reading this book I hope you now know your relationship with God has the potential to be more profound, more personal, and more loving than any organized religion on Earth currently teaches.

If you wish to develop a relationship with God's Prophet, seek the inner side of Prophet, for he is spiritually already with you. Few are able to meet the current physical incarnation and most people do not need to meet Prophet physically. Gently sing HU for a few minutes and then sing "Prophet" with love in your heart and he will respond. It may take time to recognize his presence, but it will come. The Light and Love that flows through him is the same that has flowed through all of God's true Prophets.

A more abundant life awaits you,

Prophet Del Hall III

HU — An Ancient Name For God

HU is an ancient name for God that can be sung quietly or aloud in prayer. HU has existed since the beginning of time in one form or another and is available to all regardless of religion. It is a pure way to express your love to God and give thanks for your blessings.

Singing HU (HUUUUUU pronounced "hue") serves as a tuning fork with Spirit that brings you into greater harmony with the Divine. We recommend singing HU a few minutes each day. This can bring love, joy, peace, and clarity, or help you rise to a higher view of a situation when upset or fearful.

Articles of Faith

Written by Prophet Del Hall III

1. We believe in one true God that is still living and active in our lives. He is knowable and wants a relationship with each of His children. He is the same God Jesus called FATHER, and is known by many names, including Heavenly Father. God wants a loving personal relationship with each of us, NOT one based upon fear or guilt.

2. The Holy Spirit is God's expression in all the worlds. It is in two parts, the Light and the Sound. It is through His Holy Spirit God communicates and delivers all His gifts: peace, clarity, love, joy, healings, correction, guidance, wisdom, comfort, truth, dreams, new revelations, and more.

3. God always has a chosen living Prophet to teach His ways, speak His living word, lift up Souls, and bring us closer to God. God's living Prophet is a concentrated aspect of the Holy Spirit, the Light and Sound, and is raised up

and ordained by God directly. His Prophet is empowered and authorized to share God's Light and Sound and to correct misunderstandings of His ways. There are two aspects of God's Prophet, an inner spiritual and outer physical Prophet. The inner Prophet can teach us through dreams, intuition, spiritual travel, inner communication, and his presence. The outer Prophet also teaches through his discourses, written word, and his presence. Prophet is always with us spiritually on the inner. Prophet points to and glorifies the Father.

4. God so loves the world and His children He has always had a long unbroken line of His chosen Prophets. They existed before Jesus and after Jesus. Jesus was God's Prophet and His actual SON. God's chosen Prophets are considered to be in the "role of God's Son," though NOT literally His Son. Only Jesus was literally His son. Prophets were sometimes called Paraclete. The Bible uses the word Comforter, but the original Greek word was Paraclete, which is more accurate. Paraclete implied an actual physical person who helps,

counsels, encourages, advocates, comforts, and sets free.

5. Our real and eternal self is called Soul. We are Soul; we do NOT "have" a Soul. As Soul we are literally an individualized piece of God's Holy Spirit, thereby Divine in nature. We are made of God's Light and Sound, which is actually God's Love. As an individual and uniquely experienced Soul you have free will, intelligence, imagination, opinions, clear and continuous access to Divine guidance, and immortality. As Soul we have an innate and profound spiritual growth potential. Soul has the ability to travel the Heavens spiritually with Prophet to gain truth and wisdom, and grow in love. Soul exists because God loves it.

6. We believe Soul equals Soul, in that God loves all Souls equally and each Soul has the same innate qualities and potential. Soul is neither male nor female, any particular race, nationality, or age. All Souls are children of God.

7. We believe in one eternal life as Soul. However, we believe Soul needs to incarnate

many times into a physical body to learn and grow spiritually mature. Soul's journey home to God encompasses many lifetimes. A loving God does not expect His children to learn His ways in a single lifetime.

8. We believe Soul incarnates on Earth to grow in the ability to give and receive love.

9. We believe God is more interested in two Souls experiencing love for one another than in their sexual preference.

10. It is God's will that a negative power exists to help Soul grow spiritually through challenges and hardships, thereby strengthening and maturing Soul. We are never given a challenge greater than our ability to find a solution. Soul has the ability to rise above any obstacles with God's help.

11. We study the Bible as an authentic teaching tool of God's ways, in addition to books and discourses authored by a Prophet chosen by God. We know the original Biblical writings have been altered in some cases by incorrect translations and political interference throughout the ages. God loves each of us

regardless of our errors. We do not believe in God's eternal abandonment or damnation. He would never turn His back to us for eternity.

12. Karma is the way in which the Divine accounts for our actions, words, thoughts, and attitudes. One can create positive or negative karma. Karma is a blessing used to teach us responsibility. We do not have to earn God's Love, He loves us unconditionally.

13. We do not believe that a child is born in sin, though the child may have karma from a former life. Karma, God's accounting system, explains our birth circumstances better than the concept of sin.

14. We believe that a living Prophet, including Jesus, can remove karma and sin when necessary to help us get started or to grow on the path to God. However, it is primarily our responsibility to live and grow in the ways of God, thereby not creating negative karma and sin.

15. There are four commandments of God in which we abide: First — Love God with all your heart, mind and soul; Second — Love

your neighbor as yourself. We believe the Third is, "Seek ye first the Kingdom of God, and His righteousness." We believe this means that it is primarily our responsibility to draw close to God, learn His ways, and strive to live the way God would like us to live. God's Prophets are sent to show His ways. We believe our purpose, the Fourth Commandment, is to become spiritually mature to be used by God to bless His children. Becoming a co-worker with God is our primary purpose in life and the most rewarding attainment of Soul.

16. We believe all Souls upon translation, death of the physical body, go to the higher worlds, called Heavens, Planes, or Mansions, regardless of their beliefs. The way they live life on Earth and the effort made to draw close to God impacts the area of Heaven they are to be sent. Those who draw close to a Prophet of God receive special care. We know of twelve distinct Heavens, not one. The primary abode of the Heavenly Father is in the twelfth Heaven, known as the "Ocean of Love and Mercy." We can visit God while we still

live on Earth, but only if taken by His chosen Prophet and only as Soul, not in a physical body.

17. We believe prayer is communication with God and is an extreme privilege. God hears every prayer from the heart whether or not we recognize a response. Singing an ancient name of God, HU, is our foundational prayer. It expresses love and gratitude to God and is unencumbered by words. Singing HU has the potential to raise us up in consciousness making us more receptive to God's Love, Light, and guiding Hand. After praying it is best to spend time listening to God. Prayer should never be rote or routine. We desire to trust God and surrender to His will rather than our own will.

18. We believe it is our responsibility to stay spiritually nourished. When Soul is nourished and fortified It becomes activated and we are more receptive and have clearer communication with the Divine. We believe when Jesus said "give us this day our daily bread," he meant daily spiritual nourishment, not physical bread. This can be done by

singing HU, reading scripture, praying, dream study, demonstrating gratitude for our blessings, being in a living Prophet's physical presence, or in his inner presence, or listening to his words.

19. We believe TRUTH has the power to improve every area of our lives, but only if understood, accepted, and integrated into our lives.

20. We believe God and His Prophet guide us in our sleeping dreams and awake dreams as a gift of love. God's Prophet teaches how to understand both types of dreams. All areas of our lives may be blessed by the wisdom God offers each of us directly in dreams.

21. Gratitude is extremely important on our path of love. It is literally the secret of love. Developing an attitude of gratitude is necessary to becoming spiritually mature. Recognizing and being grateful for the blessings of God in our lives is vital to building a loving and trusting relationship with God and His chosen Prophet. A relationship

with God's Prophet is THE KEY to everything good and a life more abundant.

22. We believe in being good stewards of our blessings. We recognize them as gifts of love from God and make the effort to have remembrance. Remembering our blessings helps to keep our heart open to God and builds trust in God's Love for us.

23. We believe in giving others the freedom to make their own choices and live their lives as they wish. We expect the same in return.

24. We believe the Love and Blessings of God and His Prophet are available to all who are receptive. If one desires guidance and help from Prophet, ask from the heart and sing "Prophet." He will respond. One does not need to meet Prophet physically to receive help. To be taught by Prophet it is best to attend a retreat with him in the physical. However, much can be gained by reading or listening to his teachings.

25. We have a responsibility to do our part and let God and His Prophet do their part. This responsibility brings freedom. Our goal is

to remain spiritually nourished, live in balance and harmony, and serve God as a co-worker. Anything is possible with God if we do our part. We pray to use our God-given free will in a way that our actions, thoughts, words, and attitudes testify and bear witness to the Glory and Love of God.

26. We believe there is always more to learn and grow in God's ways and truth. One cannot remain the same spiritually. One must make the effort to move forward or risk falling backward. To grow in consciousness requires change. Spiritual wisdom gained during our earthly incarnations can be taken to the other worlds when we translate, and into future lifetimes, unlike our physical possessions.

Contact Information

Guidance for a Better Life is a worldwide mentoring program provided by Prophet Del Hall III and his son Del Hall IV. Personal one-on-one mentoring at our retreat center is our premier offering and the most direct and effective way to grow spiritually. Spiritual tools, guided exercises, and in-depth discourses on the eternal teachings of God are provided to help one become more aware of and receptive to His Holy Spirit and the abundance that awaits. With this personally-tailored guidance one begins to more fully recognize God's Love daily in their lives, both the dramatic and the very subtle. Over time our mentoring reduces fear, worry, anxiety, lack of purpose, feelings of unworthiness, guilt, and confusion; replacing those negative aspects of life with an abundance of peace, clarity, joy, wisdom, love, and self-respect leading to a more personal relationship with God, more than most know is possible. We also offer our dozen books, YouTube videos, and podcast.

Guidance for a Better Life

P.O. Box 219

Lyndhurst, Virginia 22952

(540) 377-6068

contact@guidanceforabetterlife.com

www.guidanceforabetterlife.com

"A Growing Testament to the Power of God's Love One Profound Book at a Time."

If you could only read one of Prophet Del Hall's books this is the one. It is full of Keys to unlock the treasures of Heaven and bring more of God's Love into your life.

Wayshowers are God's special emissaries to Earth. Our Heavenly Father loves us so much He has never left us alone without a Wayshower to teach us His true ways. This book explores the amazing history of God's chosen and ordained Wayshowers from thirty-five thousand years ago to today through specific examples of both well-known and little-known Wayshowers.

Guidance for a Better Life retreat center has been hosting in-person mountaintop retreats at our beautiful location in the Blue Ridge Mountains of Virginia since 1990. When the pandemic began in 2020, it inspired us to get creative with how to connect with our students and new seekers. It was then our *Zoom With Prophet* meeting series was born. Some of these Zoom meetings are now being put into book form for those who could not attend.

SPECIALIZED TOPICS

Whether you wish to reconnect with a loved one who has passed, understand how you too can experience God's Light, improve your marriage, or learn how to understand your dreams, these incredible books have you covered.

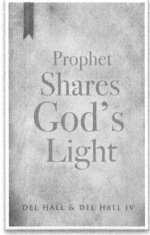

TESTIMONIES OF GOD'S LOVE SERIES

God expresses His Love every day in many different and sometimes subtle ways. Often this love goes unrecognized because the ways in which God communicates are not well known. Each of the books in this series contains fifty true stories that will help you learn to better recognize the Love of God in your life.

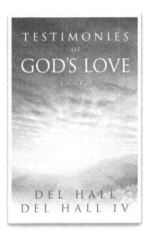
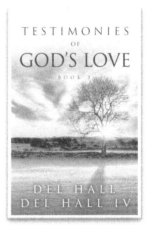
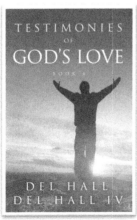

JOURNEY TO A TRUE SELF-IMAGE SERIES

This series includes intimate and unique stories that many readers will be able to personally identify with, enjoy, and learn from. They will help the reader transcend the false images people often carry about themselves — first and foremost that they are only their physical mind and body. The authors share their journeys of recognizing and coming to more fully accept their true self-image, that of Soul — an eternal child of God.

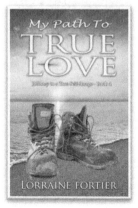

Made in the USA
Middletown, DE
23 June 2023

33309149R00156